Mildr... ... love

_B._

_2010_

An₂

Watching

Over Us

Based On The Bible

Niki Behrikis Shanahan

Niki Behrikis Shanahan

Published By:
Pete Publishing
P. O. Box 282
Tyngsborough, MA 01879

We welcome you to visit us at:

www.eternalanimals.com

Angels Are Watching Over Us

First Published 2010

ISBN-10 Digit: 0972030166
ISBN-13 Digit: 978-0-9720301-6-8

Library of Congress Control Number
2009913781

Published By:
Pete Publishing
P. O. Box 282
Tyngsborough, MA 01879

www.eternalanimals.com

Table of Contents

Chapter 1

Introduction

"Are not all angels ministering spirits sent to serve
those who will inherit salvation?"
Hebrews 1:14

There is great fascination and interest in the existence of angels. The very thought of these celestial beings traveling around from heaven to earth serving as our guardians is remarkable and exciting. Angels are seen in the movies, television, books, dreams, and visions. The stores are filled with angel themed items, and they often sit on the top of our Christmas trees. People are very captivated and intrigued with these heavenly beings.

In a 2007 Gallup, Inc. poll 75% of Americans said they believed in angels, 11% were not sure, and 14% said they do not believe in angels. This means that according to this survey, three quarters of Americans believe in angels. In this same poll, 81% of people said they believe in Heaven, and 86% believe in God. As Christians believing in the Bible, we know that angels are very real creatures, and they are as much alive and active today as they were in the Bible days.

It is comforting to know that God loves us so much that He has given us angels to watch over us and bless us. Although we might wish that angels would appear to us, we also want to remember that many times when they have appeared to people it was because of a troubling situation. I think you'd agree with me that we'd like to see them as long as we don't have to encounter trouble to achieve it.

In this book we are going to examine what the Bible teaches us about angels. Although we cannot usually see angels, they are in the company of Christians most or all the time as we will see by the Scriptures. There are almost three hundred verses referring to the existence and ministry of angels. With that much representation in the Bible, it is clear that God wants us to know about their existence, and their ministry and function relating to the believer. We know that all Scripture is useful for teaching and training in righteousness (2 Timothy 3:16). We are not left to our own wisdom or imagination on this absorbing subject.

Angels are God's faithful ministers and messengers who bring messages and give orders from God. They carry out God's will by being His agents here on earth, and they serve in a wide field of achievements. They very often come and rescue people who are in trouble. Apparently, their primary job is to look after us and protect us. They do only what God tells them to do. In the Bible they often instruct people not to be afraid of them, and they told people not to bow down or worship them.

The study of angels, as was the case with our study of animals, expands our horizons of the variety and perspective of all of God's creations.

This is an educational topic study of the Bible. We learn that angels are spirits, they don't die, they don't marry or reproduce. They were created before us, and there are many, many other interesting details. The introduction of angels meets us at the beginning of the Bible, at its close, and almost everywhere in between.

In 2 Timothy 2:15 it says we should study the Scriptures and show ourselves approved by God. There's nothing new in the Bible that wasn't there from the beginning. But rather it's our own learning curve which enables us to find new revelations in the word of God as we study it. I do not put forth theories, ideas, or opinions, but strictly the facts according to the Bible. That is why I will introduce a fact and show you the Scripture to back it up. All Scripture is from the *New International Version* (NIV) unless otherwise noted.

Having said that, I would like to point out that in the chapter called "Stories Of Angel Encounters" I am sharing stories where it is believed to be angelic intervention. It is not a fact from the Bible, but may be used as supportive evidence of angel assistance, and you may decide whether you believe them or not.

What does Angel Mean?

Baker's Evangelical Dictionary states this definition for angel.

"Superhuman or heavenly being who serves as God's messenger. Both the Hebrew *malak* and the Greek *angelos* indicate that these beings also act decisively in fulfilling God's will in the world. 'Angels' are mentioned almost three hundred times in Scripture, and are only noticeably absent from books such as Ruth, Nehemiah, Esther, the letters of John, and James."

Angels are sometimes referred to as "heavenly hosts" as is recorded in Psalm 148:2 and Luke 2:13-14. The word "hosts" in the Greek (New Testament) is *stratia*, and "hosts" in Hebrews (Old Testament) is *tsaba*, they both mean troops of angels or an organized army.

The study of angels or the branch of theology having to do with angels is called Angelology. There are two distinct groups of angels – the holy angels of God, and the evil angels who followed Satan. There is much we can learn about angels in respect to their history, rank, titles, attributes, characteristics, residence, society, employments, and pursuits.

We are going to review facts and answers to the questions we have about angels. There are specific types of angels that are covered in Chapter 3. There are only two angels in the Bible that are identified by their names, and one fallen angel. There are numerous examples of angels bringing important messages to people. We'll read about several stories of angels who rescued people from life-threatening situations.

The subject of Satan and the fallen angels will be covered. Satan was once an angel himself until he sinned and revolted against God. He took many angels with him. Somehow he was able to persuade them to follow him into a destructive path.

I think you'll enjoy hearing more current stories of angels appearing to people and assisting them in Chapter 7.

It is a great source of strength and encouragement to learn that God has blessed us with these faithful angels to watch over us. I think that someday we'll find out that angels were responsible for helping and assisting us when we were in trouble, and even when we didn't realize we were in trouble.

Chapter 2

Facts And Answers About Angels

When were the angels created?

Angels were created by God, and they were created before us. These next two verses establish that God commanded and the angels, along with all other things, "were created."

> "Praise Him, all His angels, praise Him, all His heavenly hosts. Praise Him, sun and moon, praise Him, all you shining stars. Praise Him, you highest heavens and you waters above the skies. Let them praise the name of the Lord, for He commanded and they were created."
>
> Psalm 148:2-5

> "For by Him all things were created: things in heaven and on earth, visible and invisible, whether thrones or powers or rulers or authorities; all things were created by Him and for Him."
>
> Colossians 1:16

This Scripture tells us that there isn't anything that has been made that was not made by God.

> "In the beginning was the Word, and the Word was with God, and the Word was God. He was with God in the beginning. Through Him all things were made; without Him nothing was made that has been made."
>
> John 1:1-3

Other verses that state that God created everything and everyone are Revelation 10:6, Ephesians 3:9-10, and Isaiah 40:26.

The following verses establish the fact that the angels were there to witness God when He created the earth. So we don't know exactly when they were created, but it was prior to the earth, and all that God created on the earth.

> "Then the Lord answered Job out of the storm. He said: 'Who is this that darkens my counsel with words without knowledge? Brace yourself like a man; I will question you, and you shall answer Me. 'Where were you when I laid the earth's foundation? Tell me, if you understand. Who marked off its dimensions? Surely you know! Who stretched a measuring line across it? On what were its footings set, or who laid its cornerstone – while the morning stars sang together and all the angels shouted for joy?'"
>
> Job 38:1-7

Where do angels reside?

They live in heaven and go back and forth between heaven and earth. Or you might say that it seems somewhat like an intermediate sphere between heaven and earth.

> "He then added, 'I tell you the truth, you shall see heaven open, and the angels of God ascending and descending on the Son of Man.'"
>
> John 1:51

> "Suddenly a great company of the heavenly host appeared with the angel, praising God and saying, 'Glory to God in the highest, and on earth peace to men on whom His favor rests.' When the angels had left them and gone into heaven, the shepherds said to one another, 'Let's go to Bethlehem and see this thing that has happened, which the Lord has told us about.'"
>
> Luke 2:13-15

"He had a dream in which he saw a stairway resting on the earth, with its top reaching to heaven, and the angels of God were ascending and descending on it."

Genesis 28:12

"It saves you by the resurrection of Jesus Christ, who has gone into heaven and is at God's right hand — with angels, authorities and powers in submission to Him."

1 Peter 3:21-22

They do not die.

Death for the angels is not an option. He has made them to be eternal beings.

"Jesus replied, 'The people of this age marry and are given in marriage. But those who are considered worthy of taking part in that age and in the resurrection from the dead will neither marry nor be given in marriage, and they can no longer die; for they are like the angels.'"

Luke 20:34-36

They are holy.

"If anyone is ashamed of Me and My words in this adulterous and sinful generation, the Son of Man will be ashamed of him when He comes in His Father's glory with the holy angels."

Mark 8:38 (Also, see Luke 9:26)

"The men replied, 'We have come from Cornelius the centurion. He is a righteous and God-fearing man, who is respected by all the Jewish people. A holy angel told him to have you come to his house so that he could hear what you have to say.'"

Acts 10:22

"He, too, will drink of the wine of God's fury, which has been poured full strength into the cup of His wrath. He will be tormented with burning sulfur in the presence of the holy angels and of the Lamb."

Revelation 14:10

They are innumerable.

How many angels are there? We don't know the number, but they are innumerable. The Bible says that we all have angels (Matthew 18:10), so think about how many people there are in the world, and how many angels it would take to accommodate all of us. It is apparent through Scriptures that not all of them are guardian type angels, therefore, it would be substantially more than the number of people on the earth. In addition to our guardian angels, some angels seem to have more of a praise and worship function, some fight battles, while others bring special messages.

There is a Scripture that seems to indicate that as many as one-third of the angels fell, and if that is true it means that two-thirds stayed loyal to God. Therefore, good angels would outnumber fallen angels two to one. That's certainly good news! In addition, God could have created new angels to replace the fallen ones, but we do not find proof of this in the Scriptures. This next verse states that there is an innumerable company of angels.

"But ye are come unto mount Sion, and unto the city of the living God, the Heavenly Jerusalem, and to an innumerable company of angels."

Hebrews 12:22 (KJV)

In the next verse Jesus says if He wanted to He could call twelve legions of angels to help Him. Exactly how many is twelve legions? Easton's Bible dictionary says that in the time of Christ a legion was a regiment of the Roman army that consisted of six thousand men. That would put the number of angels that Jesus had in mind up around 72,000.

"Do you think I cannot call on My Father, and He will at once put at My disposal more than twelve legions of angels?"

Matthew 26:53

Here are a couple of Scriptures indicating that there are thousands and thousands of angels.

"Then I looked and heard the voice of many angels, numbering thousands upon thousands, and ten thousand times ten thousand. They encircled the throne and the living creatures and the elders."

Revelation 5:11

"The chariots of God are twenty thousand, even thousands of angels: the Lord is among them, as in Sinai, in the holy place."

Psalm 68:17

Angels are mighty and strong.

"Praise the Lord, you His angels, you mighty ones who do His bidding, who obey His word."

Psalm 103:20

"And I saw a mighty angel proclaiming in a loud voice, 'Who is worthy to break the seals and open the scroll?'"

Revelation 5:2

"Then I saw another mighty angel coming down from heaven. He was robed in a cloud, with a rainbow above his head; his face was like the sun, and his legs were like fiery pillars."

Revelation 10:1

"Then a mighty angel picked up a boulder the size of a large millstone and threw it into the sea, and said: 'With such violence the great city of Babylon will be thrown down, never to be found again.'"

Revelation 18:21

"Bold and arrogant, these men are not afraid to slander celestial beings; yet even angels, although they are stronger and more powerful, do not bring slanderous accusations against such beings in the presence of the Lord."

2 Peter 2:11

The guards saw the angel roll back the stone where Jesus was buried, and it instilled great fear in them. They displayed their might and power, and it apparently felt like an earthquake.

"After the Sabbath, at dawn on the first day of the week, Mary Magdalene and the other Mary went to look at the tomb."

"There was a violent earthquake, for an angel of the Lord came down from heaven and, going to the tomb, rolled back the stone and sat on it. His appearance was like lightning, and his clothes were white as snow. The guards were so afraid of him that they shook and became like dead men."

Matthew 28:1-4

"... And give relief to you who are troubled, and to us as well. This will happen when the Lord Jesus is revealed from heaven in blazing fire with His powerful angels."

2 Thessalonians 1:7

Angels are often invisible.

Angels are often invisible to people as we can see from this story. At first the angel was invisible to Balaam and his two servants, however, the donkey could see the angel. Also, notice that the angel stood up for the abused donkey, and threatened to kill Balaam and spare his donkey. The angels help the animals, too!

"But God was very angry when he went, and the angel of the Lord stood in the road to oppose him. Balaam was riding on his donkey, and his two servants were with him. When the donkey saw the angel of the Lord standing in the road with a drawn sword in his hand, she turned off the road into a field. Balaam beat her to get her back on the road."

"Then the angel of the Lord stood in a narrow path between two vineyards, with walls on both sides. When the donkey saw the angel of the Lord, she pressed close to the wall, crushing Balaam's foot against it. So he beat her again."

"Then the angel of the Lord moved on ahead and stood in a narrow place where there was no room to turn, either to the right or to the left. When the donkey saw the angel of the Lord, she lay down under Balaam, and he was angry and beat her with his staff. Then the Lord opened the donkey's mouth, and she said to Balaam, 'What have I done to you to make you beat me these three times?'"

"Balaam answered the donkey, 'You have made a fool of me! If I had a sword in my hand, I would kill you right now.'"

"The donkey said to Balaam, 'Am I not your own donkey, which you have always ridden, to this day? Have I been in the habit of doing this to you?' 'No,' he said."

"Then the Lord opened Balaam's eyes, and he saw the angel of the Lord standing in the road with his sword drawn. So he bowed low and fell facedown."

"The angel of the Lord asked him, 'Why have you beaten your donkey these three times? I have come here to oppose you because your path is a reckless one before me. The donkey saw me and turned away from me these three times. If she had not turned away, I would certainly have killed you by now, but I would have spared her.'"

> Numbers 22:22-33

Angels don't marry or reproduce.

Jesus made it clear that the angels do not get married or have children.

"Jesus replied, 'The people of this age marry and are given in marriage. But those who are considered worthy of taking part in that age and in the resurrection from the dead will neither marry nor be given in marriage, and they can no longer die; for they are like the angels. They are God's children, since they are children of the resurrection.'"

> Luke 20:34-36 (Also see Matthew 22:30 and Mark 12:25)

The knowledge of angels.

They would appear to know most everything that's happening on the earth, and they're wise, have superior intelligence, and can discern between good and evil.

"And now your servant says, 'May the word of my lord the king bring me rest, for my lord the king is like an angel of God in discerning good and evil. May the Lord your God be with you.'"

2 Samuel 14:17

"Your servant Joab did this to change the present situation. My Lord has wisdom like that of an angel of God — he knows everything that happens in the land."

II Samuel 14:20

As we have seen the angels are wise and know most of what is going on in the earth. They are, however, not all-knowing as God is. We will be reading shortly that the angels would like to find out more about our salvation, so they don't have all knowledge. Also, in the next verse Jesus tells us that even the angels in heaven do not know when Jesus is coming back. No one knows the day or the hour but the Father.

"No one knows about that day or hour, not even the angels in heaven, nor the Son, but only the Father."

Matthew 24:36

What are the angels interested in learning? They want to know more about our salvation. Apparently when they found out that God had a plan of salvation for us it was a surprise to them.

"Concerning this salvation, the prophets, who spoke of the grace that was to come to you, searched intently and with the greatest care, trying to find out the time and circumstances to which the Spirit of Christ in them was pointing when he predicted the sufferings of Christ and the glories that would follow. It was revealed to them that they were not serving themselves but you, when they spoke of the things that have now been told you by those who have preached the gospel to you by the Holy Spirit sent from heaven. Even angels long to look into these things."

I Peter 1:10-12

When people get saved (born again), the angels rejoice.

Since the angels rejoice over a sinner who repents, they seem to really care about us. They're probably thinking that they're going to have some new friends someday in heaven. I guess it shouldn't be a surprise to us to know that the angels are excited when someone becomes born again, because they spend a great deal of time trying to guide us toward that goal.

"In the same way, I tell you, there is rejoicing in the presence of the angels of God over one sinner who repents."

Luke 15:10

We are not supposed to worship angels.

The angels made it clear to people that they should never worship them. They said, worship God, and told the Disciple John in Revelation 22:8-9 that he was a "fellow servant."

"At this I fell at his feet to worship him. But he said to me, 'Do not do it! I am a fellow servant with you and with your brothers who hold to the testimony of Jesus. Worship God! For the testimony of Jesus is the spirit of prophecy.'"

Revelation 19:10

"I, John, am the one who heard and saw these things. And when I had heard and seen them, I fell down to worship at the feet of the angel who had been showing them to me. But he said to me, 'Do not do it! I am a fellow servant with you and with your brothers the prophets and of all who keep the words of this book. Worship God!'"

Revelation 22:8-9

"Do not let anyone who delights in false humility and the worship of angels disqualify you for the prize. Such a person goes into great detail about what he has seen, and his unspiritual mind puffs him up with idle notions."

Colossians 2:18

We do not pray to angels.

According to the Bible, we are not to pray to angels or anyone else except to the heavenly Father through Jesus. We pray to God in Jesus Name. Here are some of the Scriptures that teach us this.

"For there is one God and one mediator between God and men, the man Christ Jesus."

1 Timothy 2:5

"Jesus answered, 'I am the way and the truth and the life. No one comes to the Father except through me.'"

John 14:6

"And I will do whatever you ask in My name, so that the Son may bring glory to the Father. You may ask Me for anything in My name, and I will do it."

John 14:13-14

"...according to His eternal purpose which He accomplished in Christ Jesus our Lord. In Him and through faith in Him we may approach God with freedom and confidence."

Ephesians 3:11-12

"Therefore, since we have a great high priest who has gone through the heavens, Jesus the Son of God, let us hold firmly to the faith we profess. For we do not have a high priest who is unable to sympathize with our weaknesses, but we have one who has been tempted in every way, just as we are — yet was without sin. Let us then approach the throne of grace with confidence, so that we may receive mercy and find grace to help us in our time of need."

Hebrews 4:14-16

"You did not choose Me, but I chose you and appointed you to go and bear fruit — fruit that will last. Then the Father will give you whatever you ask in My name."

John 15:16

"Until now you have not asked for anything in My name. Ask and you will receive, and your joy will be complete."

John 16:24

Paul shows us how to pray in the name of Jesus.

"Once when we were going to the place of prayer, we were met by a slave girl who had a spirit by which she predicted the future. She earned a great deal of money for her owners by fortune-telling. This girl followed Paul and the rest of us, shouting, 'These men are servants of the Most High God, who are telling you the way to be saved.' She kept this up for many days. Finally Paul became so troubled that he turned around and said to the spirit, 'In the name of Jesus Christ I command you to come out of her!' At that moment the spirit left her."

Acts 16:16-18

This is a story about Peter and John praying in the name of Jesus.

"One day Peter and John were going up to the temple at the time of prayer — at three in the afternoon. Now a man crippled from birth was being carried to the temple gate called Beautiful, where he was put every day to beg from those going into the temple courts. When he saw Peter and John about to enter, he asked them for money. Peter looked straight at him, as did John. Then Peter said, 'Look at us!' So the man gave them his attention, expecting to get something from them."

"Then Peter said, 'Silver or gold I do not have, but what I have I give you. In the name of Jesus Christ of Nazareth, walk.' Taking him by the right hand, he helped him up, and instantly the man's feet and ankles became strong. He jumped to his feet and began to walk. Then he went with them into the temple courts, walking and jumping, and praising God."

Acts 3:1-8

Here are other Scriptures that teach us to pray in the name of Jesus.

"Always giving thanks to God the Father for everything, in the name of our Lord Jesus Christ."

Ephesians 5:20

"And whatever you do, whether in word or deed, do it all in the name of the Lord Jesus, giving thanks to God the Father through Him."

Colossians 3:17

"Through Jesus, therefore, let us continually offer to
God a sacrifice of praise — the fruit of lips that confess
His name."

Hebrews 13:15

Angels are responsible for helping us.

God has given the angels employment and the responsibility of
helping us in an array of functions. He commands them to
minister to us, guard, deliver, protect, and encamp around us.

"Are not all angels ministering spirits sent to serve
those who will inherit salvation?"

Hebrews 1:14

"See that you do not look down on one of these little
ones. For I tell you that their angels in heaven always
see the face of my Father in heaven."

Matthew 18:10

"The angel of the Lord encamps around those who fear
Him, and He delivers them."

Psalm 34:7

"Then no harm will befall you, no disaster will come
near your tent. For He will command His angels
concerning you to guard you in all your ways; they will
lift you up in their hands, so that you will not strike
your foot against a stone."

Psalm 91:10-12

The leadership of angels.

The angels went before the chosen people as they left Egypt for
Canaan. They were told to follow the angel and obey him.

"See, I am sending an angel ahead of you to guard you along the way and to bring you to the place I have prepared. Pay attention to him and listen to what he says. Do not rebel against him; he will not forgive your rebellion, since My Name is in him. If you listen carefully to what he says and do all that I say, I will be an enemy to your enemies and will oppose those who oppose you."

Exodus 23:20-22

Another story about an angel leading someone was in Acts Chapter 10 where an angel lead a gentile man named Cornelius to Peter so he could learn about salvation. Cornelius was a devout man, he was God-fearing, and he gave generously to those in need. He also prayed regularly to God. One day he saw an angel who said his prayers and gifts to the poor have come up before God. So the angel told him to send his men to Joppa to bring back Peter. So Peter told Cornelius about Jesus, and then he was baptized in water.

Angels are spirits.

"Are not all angels ministering spirits sent to serve those who will inherit salvation?"

Hebrews 1:14

"Who maketh His angels spirits; His ministers a flaming fire."

Psalm 104:4 (KJV)

Angels have a free will.

We can see that angels have a free will since Lucifer and some of the angels made a choice to rebel against God. They had a free will to do as they pleased, and they made a bad decision.

It is also implied that those angels who remained loyal to God exercised their power of choice.

"And the angels which kept not their first estate, but left their own habitation, He hath reserved in everlasting chains under darkness unto the judgment of the great day."

Jude 1:6

"How art thou fallen from heaven, O Lucifer, son of the morning! How art thou cut down to the ground, which didst weaken the nations! For thou hast said in thine heart, I will ascend into heaven, I will exalt my throne above the stars of God: I will sit also upon the mount of the congregation, in the sides of the north: I will ascend above the heights of the clouds; I will be like the most High."

Isaiah 14:12-14

Angels have emotions.

The angels have a variety of emotions. They shout and they are happy and rejoice.

"While the morning stars sang together and all the angels shouted for joy?"

Job 38:7

"In the same way, I tell you, there is rejoicing in the presence of the angels of God over one sinner who repents."

Luke 15:10

Angels can be angered and provoked.

"Behold, I send an Angel before thee, to keep thee in the way, and to bring thee into the place which I have prepared."

"Beware of him, and obey his voice, provoke him not; for he will not pardon your transgressions: for My name is in him."

Exodus 23:20-21 (KJV)

Do Angels Rest?

Angels do rest, which probably shouldn't be too much of a surprise. We rest and there are many Scriptures that speak of God sitting on His throne and Jesus sitting at the right hand of the Father. At creation God rested on the seventh day. We shouldn't have the mindset that they are like robots. They are living, created spirit beings that have feelings and emotions.

In addition to these two verses where we see the angels sitting, we also learn in Genesis 19:1-3, which we will be reading soon, that two angels stayed the night at Lot's house. I'm sure they must have sat down and went to bed at night.

"After the Sabbath, at dawn on the first day of the week, Mary Magdalene and the other Mary went to look at the tomb. There was a violent earthquake, for an angel of the Lord came down from heaven and, going to the tomb, rolled back the stone **and sat on it**. His appearance was like lightning, and his clothes were white as snow."

Matthew 28:1-3

"The angel of the Lord came and **sat down** under the oak in Ophrah that belonged to Joash the Abiezrite, where his son Gideon was threshing wheat in a winepress to keep it from the Midianites."

Judges 6:11

Angels can be hindered or delayed in assisting us.

This next verse reveals some insight into the prayer and answer process.   Just because we don't get an answer right away doesn't mean we won't eventually.

> "But the prince of the Persian kingdom resisted me twenty-one days. Then Michael, one of the chief princes, came to help me, because I was detained there with the king of Persia."
>
> Daniel 10:13

Could a stranger be an angel?

Angels can visit us and help us without our even knowing that they are angels.   They can appear to look like people, and sometimes they are among us, and are mistaken for humans.   There may have been times in our lives when we have had contact with an angel, and did not even know it.

> "Do not forget to entertain strangers, for by so doing some people have entertained angels without knowing it."
>
> Hebrews 13:2

Angels observe us.

We also see from this next Scripture that the angels see what we're doing.   The statement "neither say before the angel" would imply that they are listening and perhaps recording our conversations.

> "Suffer not thy mouth to cause thy flesh to sin; neither say thou before the angel, that it was an error:

wherefore should God be angry at thy voice, and destroy the work of thine hands?"

Ecclesiastes 5:6 (KJV)

If we sometimes feel like we're being watched, it's probably because we are. The next verse confirms that our audience is God, Jesus, and the angels.

"I charge you, in the sight of God and Christ Jesus and the elect angels, to keep these instructions without partiality, and to do nothing out of favoritism."

1 Timothy 5:21

"For it seems to me that God has put us apostles on display at the end of the procession, like men condemned to die in the arena. We have been made a spectacle to the whole universe, to angels as well as to men."

1 Corinthians 4:9

"I tell you, whoever acknowledges Me before men, the Son of Man will also acknowledge him before the angels of God. But he who disowns Me before men will be disowned before the angels of God."

Luke 12:8-9

Angels are in submission to Jesus Christ.

Angels and all other beings, except God the Father, are in submission to Jesus Christ.

"In the past God spoke to our forefathers through the prophets at many times and in various ways, but in these last days He has spoken to us by His Son, whom He appointed heir of all things, and through whom He made the universe. The Son is the radiance of God's glory and the exact representation of His being, sustaining all things by His powerful word. After He had provided purification for sins, He sat down at the right hand of the Majesty in heaven. So He became as much superior to the angels as the name He has inherited is superior to theirs."

"For to which of the angels did God ever say,' You are my Son; today I have become your Father'? Or again, 'I will be His Father, and He will be my Son.'"

Hebrews 1:1-5

"Father, the time has come. Glorify Your Son, that your Son may glorify You. For You granted Him authority over all people that He might give eternal life to all those you have given Him."

John 17:2

"...and you have been given fullness in Christ, who is the head over every power and authority."

Colossians 2:10

"Do you think I cannot call on my Father, and He will at once put at My disposal more than twelve legions of angels?"

Matthew 26:53

"I pray also that the eyes of your heart may be enlightened in order that you may know the hope to which He has called you, the riches of His glorious inheritance in the saints, and His incomparably great power for us who believe. That power is like the working of His mighty strength, which He exerted in Christ when He raised Him from the dead and seated Him at His right hand in the heavenly realms, far above all rule and authority, power and dominion, and every title that can be given, not only in the present age but also in the one to come. And God placed all things under His feet and appointed Him to be head over everything for the church."

Ephesians 1:18-22

"And He made known to us the mystery of His will according to His good pleasure, which He purposed in Christ, to be put into effect when the times will have reached their fulfillment — to bring all things in heaven and on earth together under one head, even Christ."

Ephesians 1:9-10

"He is the image of the invisible God, the firstborn over all creation. For by Him all things were created: things in heaven and on earth, visible and invisible, whether thrones or powers or rulers or authorities; all things were created by Him and for Him. He is before all things, and in Him all things hold together. And He is the head of the body, the church; He is the beginning and the firstborn from among the dead, so that in everything He might have the supremacy. For God was pleased to have all His fullness dwell in Him, and through Him to reconcile to Himself all things, whether things on earth or things in heaven, by making peace through His blood, shed on the cross."

Colossians 1:15-20

An interesting thing to note in these verses is that Jesus went down into Hades after He rose from the dead. It says He "preached to the spirits in prison." Another point made here is that it says Noah and the ark "symbolizes baptism that now saves you."

"But in your hearts set apart Christ as Lord. Always be prepared to give an answer to everyone who asks you to give the reason for the hope that you have. But do this with gentleness and respect, keeping a clear conscience, so that those who speak maliciously against your good behavior in Christ may be ashamed of their slander. It is better, if it is God's will, to suffer for doing good than for doing evil."

"For Christ died for sins once for all, the righteous for the unrighteous, to bring you to God. He was put to death in the body but made alive by the Spirit, through whom also He went and preached to the spirits in prison who disobeyed long ago when God waited patiently in the days of Noah while the ark was being built. In it only a few people, eight in all, were saved through water, and this water symbolizes baptism that now saves you also — not the removal of dirt from the body but the pledge of a good conscience toward God. It saves you by the resurrection of Jesus Christ, who has gone into heaven and is at God's right hand — with angels, authorities and powers in submission to Him."

1 Peter 3:15-25

Because we talked about Jesus preaching to people in hades, here's another interesting point that you don't hear much about. After Jesus rose from the dead there were some bonus resurrections. It says the graves were opened, and many bodies of the saints which died arose. And they went into the holy city and appeared to many. Wow!

"The tombs broke open and the bodies of many holy people who had died were raised to life. They came out of the tombs, and after Jesus' resurrection they went into the holy city and appeared to many people."

Matthew 27:52-53

That's all Matthew wrote about it – two verses. I'd like to know what happened to these people. Did they go to heaven with Jesus or did they continue to live on earth and then die again?

They do not have "Omni" attributes.

While angels are super beings created by God there are, of course, limitations to their power, capabilities, and attributes. They are not Omnipresent, Omniscient, or Omnipotent. These are exclusive characteristics of God or what they refer to as God's "Omni Attributes." In the Bible these specific terms are not used. They are taken from Latin, but they are defined in the Scriptures.

God alone possesses the following attributes:

Omnipresent ~ This means God has the quality of being everywhere or in all places at the same time. He is unlimited with respect to space.

> "'Am I only a God nearby,' declares the Lord, 'and not a God far away? Can anyone hide in secret places so that I cannot see him?' declares the Lord. 'Do not I fill heaven and earth?' declares the Lord."
>
> Jeremiah 23:23-24

> "Where can I go from Your Spirit? Where can I flee from Your presence? If I go up to the heavens, You are there; if I make my bed in the depths, You are there. If I rise on the wings of the dawn, if I settle on the far side of the sea, even there Your hand will guide me, Your right hand will hold me fast."
>
> Psalm 139:7-10

Omniscience ~ This means God has infinite and complete knowledge, He understands everything. It includes every possible item of knowledge concerning everything or anyone who ever existed anywhere. He knows things immediately, simultaneously, and exhaustively.

"… For God is greater than our hearts, and He knows everything."

1 John 3:20

"Great is our Lord and mighty in power; His understanding has no limit."

Psalm 147:5

"For a man's ways are in full view of the Lord, and He examines all his paths."

Proverbs 5:21

Omnipotent ~ God has unlimited power or authority. He has possession of all power.

"But Jesus beheld them, and said unto them, With men this is impossible; but with God all things are possible."

Matthew 19:26

"Ah, Sovereign Lord, You have made the heavens and the earth by Your great power and outstretched arm. Nothing is too hard for You."

Jeremiah 32:17

We see from Scriptures that angels can't be everywhere at the same time, they are not all powerful, and they do not know everything. For instance, there is Scripture that says they want to know about our salvation. The angel, Gabriel, wasn't powerful enough to get an answer to prayer to Daniel. He received help from the angel, Michael.

We'll judge angels someday.

In the next verse I am assuming the Apostle Paul is talking about us judging the fallen angels, but it's not conclusive.

"If any of you has a dispute with another, dare he take it before the ungodly for judgment instead of before the saints? Do you not know that the saints will judge the world? And if you are to judge the world, are you not competent to judge trivial cases? Do you not know that we will judge angels? How much more the things of this life!"

    1 Corinthians 6:1-3

The angels come to get us and bring us to Heaven when we die.

This story gives us good insight into what happens when one of God's children dies and goes to heaven.

> "There was a rich man who was dressed in purple and fine linen and lived in luxury every day. At his gate was laid a beggar named Lazarus, covered with sores and longing to eat what fell from the rich man's table. Even the dogs came and licked his sores."

> "The time came when the beggar died and the angels carried him to Abraham's side. The rich man also died and was buried. In hell, where he was in torment, he looked up and saw Abraham far away, with Lazarus by his side. So he called to him, 'Father Abraham, have pity on me and send Lazarus to dip the tip of his finger in water and cool my tongue, because I am in agony in this fire.'"

> "But Abraham replied, 'Son, remember that in your lifetime you received your good things, while Lazarus received bad things, but now he is comforted here and you are in agony.'"

    Luke 16:19-25

This next verse is focusing on the body of Moses, but it seems clear that angels were there when he died to lead him to the Lord.

"But even the archangel Michael, when he was disputing with the Devil about the body of Moses, did not dare to bring a slanderous accusation against him, but said, 'The Lord rebuke you!'"

Jude 1:9

Jesus said that someday when we go to heaven He will introduce us to the angels. What a great invitation!

"I tell you, whoever acknowledges Me before men, the Son of Man will also acknowledge him before the angels of God."

Luke 12:8

Predicted Christ's return to earth.

At the ascension, the angels predicted Christ's personal and bodily return to earth again.

"'Men of Galilee,' they said, 'why do you stand here looking into the sky? This same Jesus, who has been taken from you into heaven, will come back in the same way you have seen Him go into heaven.'"

Acts 1:11

Angels will be with Jesus Christ when He returns.

"When the Son of Man comes in His glory, and all the angels with Him, He will sit on His throne in heavenly glory."

Matthew 25:31

"If anyone is ashamed of Me and My words in this adulterous and sinful generation, the Son of Man will be ashamed of him when He comes in His Father's glory with the holy angels."

Mark 8:38

"… And give relief to you who are troubled, and to us as well. This will happen when the Lord Jesus is revealed from heaven in blazing fire with His powerful angels."

2 Thessalonians 1:7

"Enoch, the seventh from Adam, prophesied about these men: 'See, the Lord is coming with thousands upon thousands of His holy ones to judge everyone, and to convict all the ungodly of all the ungodly acts they have done in the ungodly way, and of all the harsh words ungodly sinners have spoken against Him.'"

Jude 1:14-15

Angels praise and worship God.

One of their major functions is to worship and praise God, and they certainly appear to enjoy it.

"Praise Him, all His angels, praise Him, all His heavenly hosts."

Psalm 148:2

"And again, when God brings His firstborn into the world, He says, 'Let all God's angels worship Him.'"

Hebrews 1:6

"Suddenly a great company of the heavenly host appeared with the angel, praising God and saying, 'Glory to God in the highest, and on earth peace to men on whom His favor rests.'"

Luke 2:13-14

"Praise the Lord, you His angels, you mighty ones who do His bidding, who obey His word."

Psalm 103:20

"Above Him were seraphs, each with six wings: With two wings they covered their faces, with two they covered their feet, and with two they were flying. And they were calling to one another: 'Holy, holy, holy is the Lord Almighty; the whole earth is full of His glory.'"

Isaiah 6:2-3

"You alone are the Lord. You made the heavens, even the highest heavens, and all their starry host, the earth and all that is on it, the seas and all that is in them. You give life to everything, and the multitudes of heaven worship you."

Nehemiah 9:6

Do people become angels when they go to Heaven?

Sometimes people like to use the expression that a child, a person, or a pet is "an angel." Although it is a name of endearment, it is not literally true.

They are a different order of being. In these verses you can clearly see that God created mankind and He created angels. They are distinguished as two different types of beings. As you read these verses try to focus on the two different creatures – mankind and angels.

"What is man, that Thou art mindful of him? and the son of man, that thou visitest him? For Thou hast made him a little lower than the angels, and hast crowned him with glory and honour."

Psalm 8:4-5 (KJV)

"If I speak in the tongues of men and of angels, but have not love, I am only a resounding gong or a clanging cymbal."

1 Corinthians 13:1

In the next verse Jesus was saying that we will be "like" the angels in that we will not marry or be given in marriage. He is not saying that we will become angels.

"At the resurrection people will neither marry nor be
given in marriage; they will be like the angels in
Heaven."

Matthew 22:30

Here we see that when the beggar died the angels carried him
to Abraham. It doesn't identify Abraham as an angel.

"The time came when the beggar died and the angels
carried him to Abraham's side. The rich man also died
and was buried."

Luke 16:22

In the next verse you can see that "we" or "mankind" will
judge angels someday. Again, two different orders of beings.

"Do you not know that we will judge angels? How
much more the things of this life!"

1 Corinthians 6:3

We are "children of God" and are "equal" to the angels in
heaven. We don't change our position as "children of the
resurrection" to that of angels.

"Neither can they die any more: for they are equal unto
the angels; and are the children of God, being the
children of the resurrection."

Luke 20:36 (KJV)

In the following Scriptures we see the story about how Jesus,
Peter, John, and James saw Moses and the prophet Elijah on
the mountain. At this point, these two men were obviously
deceased many years ago. However, they appeared to them,
and they are still called "men." They are not identified as
angels, and I would think that if there were "good" people who
would qualify as becoming angels, Moses and Elijah would be
excellent candidates.

"About eight days after Jesus said this, he took Peter, John and James with Him and went up onto a mountain to pray. As He was praying, the appearance of His face changed, and His clothes became as bright as a flash of lightning. Two men, Moses and Elijah, appeared in glorious splendor, talking with Jesus. They spoke about His departure, which He was about to bring to fulfillment at Jerusalem. Peter and his companions were very sleepy, but when they became fully awake, they saw His glory and the two men standing with Him. As the men were leaving Jesus, Peter said to Him, 'Master, it is good for us to be here. Let us put up three shelters — one for You, one for Moses and one for Elijah.' (He did not know what he was saying.)"

"While he was speaking, a cloud appeared and enveloped them, and they were afraid as they entered the cloud. A voice came from the cloud, saying, 'This is My Son, whom I have chosen; listen to Him.' When the voice had spoken, they found that Jesus was alone. The disciples kept this to themselves, and told no one at that time what they had seen."

Luke 9:28-36 (also see Matthew 17 and Mark 9)

Angels are involved with visions from God.

Apparently angels have something to do with people seeing visions from God through the Holy Spirit. These verses are regarding the Apostle John's vision on Patmos, and the revelations he had there when he was "in the spirit." These were given to him by an angel or as it states, "he made it known by sending His angel to His servant John."

"The revelation of Jesus Christ, which God gave him to show His servants what must soon take place. He made it known by sending His angel to His servant John. On the Lord's Day I was in the Spirit, and I heard behind me a loud voice like a trumpet."

Revelation 1:1, 10

Churches have angels.

While the book of Revelation can be tricky to interpret, we can see that churches have angels from these Scriptures.

"The mystery of the seven stars that you saw in my right hand and of the seven golden lampstands is this: The seven stars are the angels of the seven churches, and the seven lampstands are the seven churches."

Revelation 1:20

"To the angel of the church in Smyrna write: These are the words of Him who is the First and the Last, who died and came to life again."

Revelation 2:8

"To the angel of the church in Pergamum write: These are the words of him who has the sharp, double-edged sword."

Revelation 2:12

"To the angel of the church in Thyatira write: These are the words of the Son of God, whose eyes are like blazing fire and whose feet are like burnished bronze."

Revelation 2:18

"To the angel of the church in Sardis write: These are the words of him who holds the seven spirits of God and the seven stars. I know your deeds; you have a reputation of being alive, but you are dead."

Revelation 3:1

"To the angel of the church in Philadelphia write: These are the words of him who is holy and true, who holds the key of David. What he opens no one can shut, and what he shuts no one can open."

Revelation 3:7

"To the angel of the church in Laodicea write: These are the words of the Amen, the faithful and true witness, the ruler of God's creation."

Revelation 3:14

Angels Can Eat Food.

We may never have given this idea much thought, but angels can eat food.

"The two angels arrived at Sodom in the evening, and Lot was sitting in the gateway of the city. When he saw them, he got up to meet them and bowed down with his face to the ground. 'My lords,' he said, 'please turn aside to your servant's house. You can wash your feet and spend the night and then go on your way early in the morning.' 'No,' they answered, 'we will spend the night in the square. But he insisted so strongly that they did go with him and entered his house. He prepared a meal for them, baking bread without yeast, and they ate."

Genesis 19:1-3

Angels can assist God in the healing process.

"Now there is at Jerusalem by the sheep market a pool, which is called in the Hebrew tongue Bethesda, having five porches. In these lay a great multitude of impotent folk, of blind, halt, withered, waiting for the moving of the water. For an angel went down at a certain season into the pool, and troubled the water: whosoever then first after the troubling of the water stepped in was made whole of whatsoever disease he had."

John 5:2-4 (KJV)

As we have seen in this chapter, the angels were created by God and reside in heaven. They travel back and forth from heaven to earth. They are holy, innumerable, they don't die, don't marry or reproduce. They know most of what is going on in the earth. They are spirits with a free will, emotions, and they worship God, help us, and are in submission to Jesus Christ.

Chapter 3

Names And Types Of Angels

Are angels identified by name in the Bible?

There are two specific angels identified in the Bible by name. They are Michael and Gabriel. In addition, Lucifer, the fallen angel is identified and we will be covering him later.

Michael

The Hebrew name Michael means "who is like God." The angel Michael is mentioned in Jude, Daniel, and Revelation. Michael is identified as an Archangel, he has angels that work under him, and he is a warrior.

> "But even the archangel Michael, when he was disputing with the Devil about the body of Moses, did not dare to bring a slanderous accusation against him, but said, 'The Lord rebuke you!'"
>
> Jude 1:9

In this next verse we see that the angel Gabriel was trying to bring Daniel a message, and when he experienced difficulty, it was necessary for Michael to assist him. It appears that the reason Gabriel needed help when things got rough is because he is more of a messenger whereas Michael is more of a warrior. Michael is also identified as "one of the chief princes." This shows us something of the nature of things transpiring in the unseen world.

> "But the prince of the Persian kingdom resisted me twenty-one days. Then Michael, one of the chief princes, came to help me, because I was detained there with the king of Persia."
>
> Daniel 10:13

From this verse and many others we can see that there are ranks and orders among the angels. It says "Michael and his angels" fought against the dragon.

> "And there was war in heaven. Michael and his angels fought against the dragon, and the dragon and his angels fought back."
>
> Revelation 12:7

Michael is the patron angel of Israel, and he appears to be involved in end time activities. Here, as in Daniel 10:13,

Michael is referred to as a "prince." This is prophecy regarding the end times.

> "At that time Michael, the great prince who protects your people, will arise. There will be a time of distress such as has not happened from the beginning of nations until then. But at that time your people — everyone whose name is found written in the book — will be delivered. Multitudes who sleep in the dust of the earth will awake: some to everlasting life, others to shame and everlasting contempt. Those who are wise will shine like the brightness of the heavens, and those who lead many to righteousness, like the stars for ever and ever."
>
> Daniel 12:1-3

Gabriel

The Hebrew word Gabriel means "man of God." He is mentioned in the book of Luke and Daniel. Gabriel seems to have the function of being a messenger, but not just a messenger – he gives a prophetic message of things that would take place in the future. He gives important messages from God to people. He must be a high level angel because he was entrusted with the job of bringing two special messages – one was the birth of John the Baptist, and the other was the birth of Jesus Christ. John the Baptist was the forerunner of Jesus, and he preached everywhere he went. He is the one who baptized Jesus in water. Notice that the appearance of this angel, as well as the message, was an answer to Zechariah's prayer.

> "Then an angel of the Lord appeared to him, standing at the right side of the altar of incense. When Zechariah saw him, he was startled and was gripped with fear. But the angel said to him: 'Do not be afraid, Zechariah; **your prayer has been heard**. Your wife Elizabeth will bear you a son, and you are to give him the name John. He will be a joy and delight to you, and many will

rejoice because of his birth, for he will be great in the sight of the Lord. He is never to take wine or other fermented drink, and he will be filled with the Holy Spirit even from birth.'"

"'Many of the people of Israel will he bring back to the Lord their God. And he will go on before the Lord, in the spirit and power of Elijah, to turn the hearts of the fathers to their children and the disobedient to the wisdom of the righteous — to make ready a people prepared for the Lord.' Zechariah asked the angel, 'How can I be sure of this? I am an old man and my wife is well along in years.' The angel answered, 'I am Gabriel. I stand in the presence of God, and I have been sent to speak to you and to tell you this good news."

Luke 1:11-19

"In the sixth month, God sent the angel Gabriel to Nazareth, a town in Galilee to a virgin pledged to be married to a man named Joseph, a descendant of David. The virgin's name was Mary. The angel went to her and said, 'Greetings, you who are highly favored! The Lord is with you.'"

'Mary was greatly troubled at his words and wondered what kind of greeting this might be. But the angel said to her, 'Do not be afraid, Mary, you have found favor with God. You will be with child and give birth to a son, and you are to give Him the name Jesus. He will be great and will be called the Son of the Most High. The Lord God will give Him the throne of His father David, and He will reign over the house of Jacob forever; His kingdom will never end.'"

"'How will this be,' Mary asked the angel, 'since I am a virgin?' The angel answered, 'The Holy Spirit will come upon you, and the power of the Most High will overshadow you. So the holy one to be born will be called the Son of God. Even Elizabeth your relative is going to have a child in her old age, and she who was said to be barren is in her sixth month. For nothing is impossible with God.' 'I am the Lord's servant,' Mary answered. 'May it be to me as you have said.' Then the angel left her."

Luke 1:26-38

Here Gabriel is interpreting a dream for Daniel.

"And I heard a man's voice from the Ulai calling, 'Gabriel, tell this man the meaning of the vision.'"

Daniel 8:16

"While I was speaking and praying, confessing my sin and the sin of my people Israel and making my request to the Lord my God for His holy hill – while I was still in prayer, Gabriel, the man I had seen in the earlier vision, came to me in swift flight about the time of the evening sacrifice. He instructed me and said to me, 'Daniel, I have now come to give you insight and understanding. As soon as you began to pray, an answer was given, which I have come to tell you, for you are highly esteemed. Therefore, consider the message and understand the vision.'"

"Seventy 'sevens' are decreed for your people and your holy city to finish transgression, to put an end to sin, to atone for wickedness, to bring in everlasting righteousness, to seal up vision and prophecy and to anoint the most holy."

"Know and understand this: From the issuing of the decree to restore and rebuild Jerusalem until the Anointed One, the ruler, comes, there will be seven 'sevens,' and sixty-two 'sevens.' It will be rebuilt with streets and a trench, but in times of trouble. After the sixty-two 'sevens,' the Anointed One will be cut off and will have nothing. The people of the ruler who will come will destroy the city and the sanctuary. The end will come like a flood: War will continue until the end, and desolations have been decreed. He will confirm a covenant with many for one 'seven.' In the middle of the 'seven' he will put an end to sacrifice and offering. And on a wing *of the temple* he will set up an abomination that causes desolation, until the end that is decreed is poured out on him."

   Daniel 9:20-27

Types of Angels

The types of angels are Seraphim, Cherubim or Cherub, and Archangels. Most people believe that the Living Creatures also referred to as the Four Beasts are some type of angel.

Archangel

Archangel comes from the Greek word *archaggelos* and means a chief angel. Michael is identified as an archangel.

"But even the archangel Michael, when he was disputing with the Devil about the body of Moses, did not dare to bring a slanderous accusation against him, but said, 'The Lord rebuke you!'"

   Jude 1:9

"For the Lord Himself will come down from heaven, with a loud command, with the voice of the archangel and with the trumpet call of God, and the dead in Christ will rise first."

   1 Thessalonians 4:16

Seraphim

Here are two verses where the angels called Seraphim with six wings are mentioned and described. They seem to lead heaven in worship of God, and ascribe holiness and sovereignty to Him.

"In the year that king Uzziah died I saw also the Lord sitting upon a throne, high and lifted up, and His train filled the temple."

"Above it stood the seraphims: each one had six wings; with twain he covered his face, and with twain he covered his feet, and with twain he did fly."

"And one cried unto another, and said, Holy, holy, holy, is the Lord of hosts: the whole earth is full of His glory."

Isaiah 6:1-3 (KJV)

"Then flew one of the seraphims unto me, having a live coal in his hand, which he had taken with the tongs from off the altar."

Isaiah 6:6 (KJV)

Making note of an interesting similarity.

There is a curious similarity that I'd like to point out in the next two categories which are the Cherubim/Cherub and The Living Creatures also referred to as The Four Beasts. When you read the description of the Cherubim you will see that they have four faces. The four faces are of a cherub, a man, a lion and an eagle.

When you read the description of The Living Creatures/The Four Beasts it says there were four of them (four creatures). Described are four different creatures as opposed to four faces on one creature called the Cherubim. Of The Four Living Creatures, one is like a lion, one like a ox, one a man, and the fourth like a flying eagle.

Both the Cherubim and The Living Creatures are described with appearances much like some type of animal.

Cherubim or Cherub (They have four faces)

Here are a few verses that tell us about the type of angel called Cherubim or Cherub which have wings. It seems that their primary function is guarding. They are mentioned in the books of Psalm, Samuel, Genesis, Exodus, and Ezekiel. God is often described as sitting on a throne supported by Cherubim.

The first time angels are mentioned in the Bible is after Adam and Eve sinned. Because they disobeyed God, they were thrown out of the Garden of Eden. It was the Cherubim angels that guarded the entrance to keep them out with a flaming sword flashing back and forth. They were guarding "the tree of life."

"After He drove the man out, He placed on the east side of the Garden of Eden cherubim and a flaming sword flashing back and forth to guard the way to the tree of life."

Genesis 3:24

"The cherubim had their wings spread upward, overshadowing the cover with them. The cherubim faced each other, looking toward the cover."

Exodus 37:9

"Now the cherubim were standing on the south side of the temple when the man went in, and a cloud filled the inner court."

Ezekiel 10:3

"The sound of the wings of the cherubim could be heard as far away as the outer court, like the voice of God Almighty when He speaks."

Ezekiel 10:5

"Each of the cherubim had four faces: One face was that of a cherub, the second the face of a man, the third the face of a lion, and the fourth the face of an eagle."

Ezekiel 10:14

"He parted the heavens and came down; dark clouds were under His feet. He mounted the cherubim and flew; He soared on the wings of the wind."

Psalm 18:9-10

The next three verses all tell us that God sits enthroned between the cherubim.

"Hear us, O Shepherd of Israel, You who lead Joseph like a flock; You who sit enthroned between the cherubim, shine forth."

Psalm 80:1

"The Lord reigns, let the nations tremble; He sits enthroned between the cherubim, let the earth shake."

Psalm 99:1

"So the people sent men to Shiloh, and they brought back the ark of the covenant of the Lord Almighty, who is enthroned between the cherubim. And Eli's two sons, Hophni and Phinehas, were there with the ark of the covenant of God."

1 Samuel 4:4

Here are more Scriptures regarding the Cherubim.

"I looked, and I saw the likeness of a throne of sapphire above the expanse that was over the heads of the cherubim. The Lord said to the man clothed in linen, 'Go in among the wheels beneath the cherubim. Fill your hands with burning coals from among the cherubim and scatter them over the city.' And as I watched, he went in."

"Now the cherubim were standing on the south side of the temple when the man went in, and a cloud filled the inner court. Then the glory of the Lord rose from above the cherubim and moved to the threshold of the temple. The cloud filled the temple, and the court was full of the radiance of the glory of the Lord. The sound of the wings of the cherubim could be heard as far away as the outer court, like the voice of God Almighty when He speaks."

"When the Lord commanded the man in linen, 'Take fire from among the wheels, from among the cherubim,' the man went in and stood beside a wheel. Then one of the cherubim reached out his hand to the fire that was among them. He took up some of it and put it into the hands of the man in linen, who took it and went out. (Under the wings of the cherubim could be seen what looked like the hands of a man.)"

"I looked, and I saw beside the cherubim four wheels, one beside each of the cherubim; the wheels sparkled like chrysolite. As for their appearance, the four of them looked alike; each was like a wheel intersecting a wheel. As they moved, they would go in any one of the four directions the cherubim faced; the wheels did not turn about as the cherubim went."

"The cherubim went in whatever direction the head faced, without turning as they went. Their entire bodies, including their backs, their hands and their wings, were completely full of eyes, as were their four wheels. I heard the wheels being called 'the whirling wheels.' Each of the cherubim had four faces: One face was that of a cherub, the second the face of a man, the third the face of a lion, and the fourth the face of an eagle."

"Then the cherubim rose upward. These were the living creatures I had seen by the Kebar River. When the cherubim moved, the wheels beside them moved; and when the cherubim spread their wings to rise from the ground, the wheels did not leave their side. When the cherubim stood still, they also stood still; and when the cherubim rose, they rose with them, because the spirit of the living creatures was in them."

"Then the glory of the Lord departed from over the threshold of the temple and stopped above the cherubim. While I watched, the cherubim spread their wings and rose from the ground, and as they went, the wheels went with them. They stopped at the entrance to the east gate of the Lord's house, and the glory of the God of Israel was above them."

"These were the living creatures I had seen beneath the God of Israel by the Kebar River, and I realized that they were cherubim. Each had four faces and four wings, and under their wings was what looked like the hands of a man. Their faces had the same appearance as those I had seen by the Kebar River. Each one went straight ahead."

Ezekiel 10:1-22

Living Creatures or The Four Beasts (There are four creatures)

The Living Creatures or The Four Beasts are spoken of in the book of Revelation. Most people believe they are angels.

"Also before the throne there was what looked like a sea of glass, clear as crystal. In the center, around the throne, were four living creatures, and they were covered with eyes, in front and in back. The first living creature was like a lion, the second was like an ox, the third had a face like a man, the fourth was like a flying eagle. Each of the four living creatures had six wings and was covered with eyes all around, even under his wings. Day and night they never stop saying: 'Holy, holy, holy is the Lord God Almighty, who was, and is, and is to come.' Whenever the living creatures give glory, honor and thanks to Him who sits on the throne and who lives forever and ever, the twenty-four elders fall down before Him who sits on the throne, and worship Him who lives for ever and ever. They lay their crowns before the throne and say: 'You are worthy, our Lord and God, to receive glory and honor and power, for You created all things, and by Your will they were created and have their being.'"

Revelation 4:6-11

"When the creatures moved, I heard the sound of their wings, like the roar of rushing waters, like the voice of the Almighty, like the tumult of an army. When they stood still, they lowered their wings. Then there came a voice from above the expanse over their heads as they stood with lowered wings. Above the expanse over their heads was what looked like a throne of sapphire, and high above on the throne was a figure like that of a man. I saw that from what appeared to be His waist up He looked like glowing metal, as if full of fire, and that from there down He looked like fire; and brilliant light surrounded Him. Like the appearance of a rainbow in the clouds on a rainy day, so was the radiance around Him. This was the appearance of the likeness of the glory of the Lord. When I saw it, I fell facedown, and I heard the voice of one speaking."

Ezekiel 1:24-28

Ranks and Organization of Angels

The vast number of angels are highly organized and ranked according to class and position. They appear to form the power or dominion of a hierarchy. They have differing ranks, stations, attributes, and employments. The fact that there is organization in heaven is evident in many Scriptures. In these verses we see that there was a set time or protocol when the angels would present themselves to the Lord. Even Satan was able to wiggle his way into this meeting. He apparently knows when the angels are going to appear before God.

"One day the angels came to present themselves before the Lord, and Satan also came with them."

Job 1:6

"On another day the angels came to present themselves before the Lord, and Satan also came with them to present himself before Him."

Job 2:1

This Scripture tells us of thrones, powers, rulers, and authorities in the order of angels.

"For by Him all things were created: things in heaven and on earth, visible and invisible, whether thrones or powers or rulers or authorities; all things were created by Him and for Him."

Colossians 1:16

Michael has his own army, and "the dragon" which is Satan, fought back with his fallen angels. This is end time prophecy from the book of Revelation.

> "And there was war in heaven. Michael and his angels
> fought against the dragon, and the dragon and his
> angels fought back."

>   Revelation 12:7

This verse identifies Michael as an archangel. The Greek word
"arche" means first or leader. It seems that at the present time
the angels have to give Satan a certain amount of respect or
acknowledgement.

> "But even the archangel Michael, when he was
> disputing with the Devil about the body of Moses, did
> not dare to bring a slanderous accusation against him,
> but said, 'The Lord rebuke you!'"

>   Jude 1:9

The fact that it states that Michael is "one of the chief princes"
implies that there are other princes and high ranking angels, as
well as lower ranking angels. Notice the wording "Persian
kingdom" and "king of Persia." These are obviously titles
recognized in the spirit world.

> "But the prince of the Persian kingdom resisted me
> twenty-one days. Then Michael, one of the chief
> princes, came to help me, because I was detained there
> with the king of Persia."

>   Daniel 10:13

The Apostle Paul talks about rulers and authorities, both of
good and evil angels in these verses. It also lays out the
foundation for their organizational classifications.

> "His intent was that now, through the church, the
> manifold wisdom of God should be made known to the
> rulers and authorities in the heavenly realms."

>   Ephesians 3:10

This next verse suggests that even though Satan and the fallen
angels are estranged from God, they still have their form of

organization and ranks. There are spiritual forces behind these evil fallen angels. Their purpose is to carry out the schemes of Satan and to oppose God. How, you might ask? By tempting people, deceiving them, and deluding them into eternal damnation.

The problem is that we can't see them. Remember some of those pictures you'd see of a good angel with a halo, wings, and dressed in white who would be on someone's shoulder? On the other shoulder would be the Devil with horns and a pitchfork. This was supposed to represent your conscience. Well, it may have seemed funny, but it is an interesting visual of our inner conflicts. Spiritual forces of good and evil are real.

> "For our struggle is not against flesh and blood, but against the rulers, against the authorities, against the powers of this dark world and against the spiritual forces of evil in the heavenly realms."
>
> Ephesians 6:12

This verse explains that there's an organization of rule, authority, power, dominion, and titles.

> "Far above all rule and authority, power and dominion, and every title that can be given, not only in the present age but also in the one to come."
>
> Ephesians 1:21

> "Who has gone into heaven and is at God's right hand — with angels, authorities and powers in submission to Him."
>
> 1 Peter 3:22

Angels are organized to go into battle.

"And there was war in heaven. Michael and his angels fought against the dragon, and the dragon and his angels fought back."

Revelation 12:7

Here we see again that there are various powers and authorities, and Jesus is the head over any and all authority under God.

"... and you have been given fullness in Christ, who is the head over every power and authority."

Colossians 2:10

In this verse, we see that Jesus has "disarmed the powers and authorities" by His death on the cross, and through His resurrection.

"And having disarmed the powers and authorities, He made a public spectacle of them, triumphing over them by the cross."

Colossians 2:15

"Then the end will come, when He hands over the kingdom to God the Father after He has destroyed all dominion, authority and power."

1 Corinthians 15:24

The fact that Jesus said He could call twelve legions of angels suggests that they are organized into armies and ranks. It certainly appears that they are coordinated for efficient dispatch at any moment. This can only be achieved by leadership and organization.

"Do you think I cannot call on My Father, and He will at once put at My disposal more than twelve legions of angels?"

Matthew 26:53

Here are three different times that Jesus called Satan "the prince of this world." He is the prince of this world temporarily until Jesus comes back. However, he has no authority over Christians. It clearly places Satan as the leader of the evil spiritual world.

"Now is the time for judgment on this world; now the prince of this world will be driven out."

John 12:31

"I will not speak with you much longer, for the prince of this world is coming. He has no hold on Me."

John 14:30

"… and in regard to judgment, because the prince of this world now stands condemned."

John 16:11

Satan is described as "the prince of the power of the air" which is probably another expression meaning the prince of this world.

"Wherein in time past ye walked according to the course of this world, according to the prince of the power of the air, the spirit that now worketh in the children of disobedience."

Ephesians 2:2 (KJV)

Satan also called "the dragon" has his own army of fallen angels that report to him. Again, placing Satan as the leader or head of the evil spiritual world or kingdom.

"And there was war in heaven: Michael and his angels fought against the dragon; and the dragon fought and his angels."

Revelation 12:7

"Then shall He say also unto them on the left hand, Depart from Me, ye cursed, into everlasting fire, prepared for the Devil and his angels."

Matthew 25:41

What is the rank of angels compared to us?

At least at the present time we are a little lower in rank than the angels.

"What is man, that Thou art mindful of him? and the son of man, that thou visitest him? For Thou hast made him a little lower than the angels, and hast crowned him with glory and honor."

Psalm 8:4-5 (KJV)

In the next verse the angel tells the Apostle John that he is a "fellow servant" which would place our rank close to that of the angels even at the present time.

"At this I fell at his feet to worship him. But he said to me, 'Do not do it! I am a fellow servant with you and with your brothers who hold to the testimony of Jesus. Worship God! For the testimony of Jesus is the spirit of prophecy.'"

Revelation 19:10

It appears that in Heaven we will be equal with the angels, since Jesus said in reference to heaven "they are equal unto the angels."

"Neither can they die any more: for they are equal unto the angels; and are the children of God, being the children of the resurrection."

Luke 20:36 (KJV)

What do the angels look like?

As we have seen from all this information on angels, they can be invisible, often they look like men, and some are described with wings and faces like men, ox, lion, and eagles. They are sometimes described as having an appearance like lightning as in the next verses.

> "After the Sabbath, at dawn on the first day of the week, Mary Magdalene and the other Mary went to look at the tomb. There was a violent earthquake, for an angel of the Lord came down from heaven and, going to the tomb, rolled back the stone and sat on it. His appearance was like lightning, and his clothes were white as snow."
>
> Matthew 28:1-3

I thought it was interesting that it said the angel rolled back the stone "and sat on it." It looks like they relax and rest sometimes, too.

Although the Scriptures often do not describe what the angels look like, it is always clear that the people know they are angels. They do not seem to be confused about whether it's an angel or a person. Apparently, they must have a certain radiance and bright appearance to them.

We read earlier in Revelation 10:1 that an angel had a face like the sun, and his legs were fiery pillars. Also, we see from this next verse that God makes them a "flaming fire."

> "Who maketh His angels spirits; His ministers a flaming fire."
>
> Psalm 104:4 (KJV)

They can look like ordinary people as we're told in Hebrews 13:2 that we should not forget to entertain strangers, because they could be angels. This means they are not always distinguishable from people. Also, in Daniel 9:20-27 which we will be reading soon, Gabriel is mentioned as, "Gabriel, the man I had seen in the earlier vision."

Many of you may be wondering why we don't hear about female and child angels in the Bible. The fact is that there are no instances in the Bible of female and child angels. They all seem to have the appearance of a man, a masculine gender, or some other angelic type of creature with wings and various descriptions. Interestingly, most of the angels depicted in movies, pictures, and commercial items are female or little cupid-like angels. Many of them look more like the good witch in The Wizard Of Oz, somewhat like the Christmas tree toppers you see.

It may be that in the Bible days male angels would have been the expected visitors, and so perhaps God arranged it that way. There seems to be no distinction of sex among the angels. I personally believe that they are both male and female in appearance, particularly when you consider that Jesus said we'll be like the angels when we get to heaven in that we will not marry. Also, the Apostle Paul had said in Galatians 3:28 that there's neither Jew nor Greek or male or female in heaven or in the spirit realm. It seems that angels are not distinguished by sex, but simply appear as males.

In the case of the Cherubim and The Living Creatures they seem to take on more of an appearance of an animal with wings, and faces that look like an ox, lion, and an eagle. And, I might add, these animal-like angel beings have very close proximity to God! In Psalm 80:1, 99:1, and 1 Samuel 4:4 it says that God sits between them. The Living Creatures are also around the throne of God as in Revelation 4:6-11, and they never stop saying "Holy, holy, holy is the Lord God Almighty, who was, and is, and is to come."

Some angels have wings, but others may be able to fly without wings. I'm sure that with God it isn't necessary for a being to have wings in order to fly, but they might. There are a couple of verses I'd like to point out where angels are flying, but are not described as having wings.

> "While I was still in prayer, Gabriel, the man I had seen in the earlier vision, came to me in swift flight about the time of the evening sacrifice."
>
> Daniel 9:21

> "Then I saw another angel flying in midair, and he had the eternal gospel to proclaim to those who live on the earth — to every nation, tribe, language and people."
>
> Revelation 14:6

In the Garden of Eden Satan, the fallen angel, appeared as a serpent. Apparently, he can change his appearance as the next Scripture says he can masquerade as an angel of light.

> "And no wonder, for Satan himself masquerades as an angel of light. It is not surprising, then, if his servants masquerade as servants of righteousness. Their end will be what their actions deserve."
>
> 2 Corinthians 11:14-15

So the bottom line is that they could take on many appearances.

To summarize, we know of two angels who are identified by name – Gabriel and Michael. We learned that there are various types of angels. They are Archangels, Seraphim, Cherubim, and The Living Creatures. And they take on various appearances.

Chapter 4

Angel Messengers

Angels bringing special messages

The angel told Mary about Jesus.

There are several stories of angels bringing special messages from God to people. It's important to realize that the angels are not simply bringing messages to people – they are in many cases prophesying what will happen in the future. This prophetic capability has been given to the angels by God.

In this story Mary has found favor with God, and is instructed by the angel, Gabriel, that she will conceive and give birth to our Lord. If that wasn't enough of a shock for Mary to hear, Gabriel also told her that she might want to check in with her relative, Elizabeth, because she's in her sixth month of pregnancy even though she is up in age.

"In the sixth month of Elizabeth's pregnancy, God sent the angel Gabriel to Nazareth, a village in Galilee, to a virgin named Mary. She was engaged to be married to a man named Joseph, a descendant of King David. Gabriel appeared to her and said, 'Greetings, favored woman! The Lord is with you.'"

"Confused and disturbed, Mary tried to think what the angel could mean. 'Don't be afraid, Mary,' the angel told her, 'for you have found favor with God! You will conceive and give birth to a Son, and you will name Him Jesus. He will be very great and will be called the Son of the Most High. The Lord God will give Him the throne of His ancestor David. And He will reign over Israel forever; His Kingdom will never end!'"

"Mary asked the angel, 'But how can this happen? I am a virgin.' The angel replied, 'The Holy Spirit will come

upon you, and the power of the Most High will
overshadow you. So the baby to be born will be holy,
and He will be called the Son of God. What's more,
your relative Elizabeth has become pregnant in her old
age! People used to say she was barren, but she's now
in her sixth month. For nothing is impossible with
God.'"

"Mary responded, 'I am the Lord's servant. May
everything you have said about me come true.' And
then the angel left her."

Luke 1:26-38

The angel told the shepherds about the coming Messiah.

The angel told the shepherds about the coming of the Messiah.

"And there were shepherds living out in the fields
nearby, keeping watch over their flocks at night. An
angel of the Lord appeared to them, and the glory of the
Lord shone around them, and they were terrified. But
the angel said to them, 'Do not be afraid. I bring you
good news of great joy that will be for all the people.
Today in the town of David a Savior has been born to
you; He is Christ the Lord. This will be a sign to you:
You will find a baby wrapped in cloths and lying in a
manger.'"

"Suddenly a great company of the heavenly host
appeared with the angel, praising God and saying,
'Glory to God in the highest, and on earth peace to men
on whom His favor rests.'"

Luke 2:8-14

An angel told Joseph to escape to Egypt with Jesus.

Herod wanted to find out who the messiah was and kill him, so the angel told Joseph to take baby Jesus and Mary and flee to Egypt.

> "When they had gone, an angel of the Lord appeared to Joseph in a dream. 'Get up,' he said, 'take the Child and His mother and escape to Egypt. Stay there until I tell you, for Herod is going to search for the Child to kill Him.' So he got up, took the Child and His mother during the night and left for Egypt, where he stayed until the death of Herod. And so was fulfilled what the Lord had said through the prophet: 'Out of Egypt I called My Son.'"
>
> Matthew 2:13-15

The angel told the women that Jesus was alive.

After Jesus was crucified and rose from the grave, the angel told the women that He was alive. This is the great Easter story that Jesus is not in the grave. He has risen! He is alive!

> "The angel said to the women, 'Do not be afraid, for I know that you are looking for Jesus, who was crucified. He is not here; He has risen, just as He said. Come and see the place where He lay. Then go quickly and tell His disciples: 'He has risen from the dead and is going ahead of you into Galilee. There you will see Him. Now I have told you.'"
>
> Matthew 28:5-7

Angels bring the law to Moses and Israel.

God gave the law to Israel and Moses, and the angels were instrumental in this.

> "What, then, was the purpose of the law? It was added because of transgressions until the Seed to whom the promise referred had come. The law was put into effect through angels by a mediator."
>
> Galations 3:19

> "You who have received the law that was put into effect through angels but have not obeyed it."
>
> Acts 7:53

Gabriel brought Daniel a message.

> "While I was speaking and praying, confessing my sin and the sin of my people Israel and making my request to the Lord my God for His holy hill – while I was still in prayer, Gabriel, the man I had seen in the earlier vision, came to me in swift flight about the time of the evening sacrifice. He instructed me and said to me, 'Daniel, I have now come to give you insight and understanding. As soon as you began to pray, an answer was given, which I have come to tell you, for you are highly esteemed. Therefore, consider the message and understand the vision:'"
>
> Daniel 9:20-23

An angel told of the birth of Sampson.

Most of us remember Bible stories of Sampson, the man with enormous strength given by God. He was taken in by Delilah who found out the secret of his strength – he was never supposed to cut his hair. This is the story about how an angel appeared to Sampson's mother to tell her about his birth.

"The angel of the Lord appeared to her and said, 'You are sterile and childless, but you are going to conceive and have a son. Now see to it that you drink no wine or other fermented drink and that you do not eat anything unclean, because you will conceive and give birth to a son. No razor may be used on his head, because the boy is to be a Nazirite, set apart to God from birth, and he will begin the deliverance of Israel from the hands of the Philistines.'"

"Then the woman went to her husband and told him, 'A man of God came to me. He looked like an angel of God, very awesome. I didn't ask him where he came from, and he didn't tell me his name. But he said to me, 'You will conceive and give birth to a son. Now then, drink no wine or other fermented drink and do not eat anything unclean, because the boy will be a Nazirite of God from birth until the day of his death.'"

Judges 13:3-7

As we have seen, the angels bless us in many ways. They bring special messages, prophesy future events, help and rescue us, and do only as God tells them to do.

Chapter 5

Activating Angelic Intervention

How do we activate angelic intervention? We activate it through prayer and faith. We already learned that we are always to pray to the Father through Jesus, so we know that we should never attempt to contact angels to activate their assistance. To make it easier to grasp, I would describe the process as a "Relay." It operates like this:

1. We pray to God.

2. God receives the request.

3. God dispatches the angels to help us.

4. Angels arrive to help.

5. Answer received.

Obviously there is a matter of time involved in the process. Sometimes it isn't God's time for the answer. However, there are times when we really need fast help. Let's say that you are driving in your car and suddenly you must avoid an accident. You don't have time for a long fancy prayer. So you say "Jesus help me." The question comes to mind, how can God send help in seconds. For one thing time is no obstacle for God. And, secondly, I recall the Scripture where God says "before you call, I will answer." He is God and knows all things so He knows what's coming up before we do.

Examples of angels helping people in the Bible.

Notice in the following story that an angel rescued the Apostle Peter out of prison for preaching the gospel. Here's the key to the answered prayer, it says "So Peter was kept in prison, but the church was earnestly praying to God for him." Then the second story is about Daniel and you'll see that it says "he had trusted his God." The third story is about Paul who was shipwrecked, and an angel appeared to him to tell him that he, and all those on the ship would be saved.

The disciple, Peter, was rescued from prison.

"It was about this time that King Herod arrested some who belonged to the church, intending to persecute them. He had James, the brother of John, put to death with the sword. When he saw that this pleased the Jews, he proceeded to seize Peter also. This happened during the Feast of Unleavened Bread. After arresting him, he put him in prison, handing him over to be guarded by four squads of four soldiers each. Herod intended to bring him out for public trial after the Passover. **So Peter was kept in prison, but the church was earnestly praying to God for him.**"

"The night before Herod was to bring him to trial, Peter was sleeping between two soldiers, bound with two chains, and sentries stood guard at the entrance. Suddenly an angel of the Lord appeared and a light shone in the cell. He struck Peter on the side and woke him up. 'Quick, get up!' he said, and the chains fell off Peter's wrists."

"Then the angel said to him, 'Put on your clothes and sandals' And Peter did so. 'Wrap your cloak around you and follow me,' the angel told him. Peter followed him out of the prison, but he had no idea that what the angel was doing was really happening; he thought he was seeing a vision. They passed the first and second guards and came to the iron gate leading to the city. It opened for them by itself, and they went through it. When they had walked the length of one street, suddenly the angel left him."

Acts 12:1-10

Did you notice that it said when they came to the iron gate "it opened for them by itself." I'd say that was the work of an invisible angel. I actually never noticed that point about the gate before. I also thought it was interesting that the angel struck Peter on the side, and then told him to put his sandals on and his cloak so he wouldn't get cold.

"Then Peter came to himself and said, 'Now I know without a doubt that the Lord sent His angel and rescued me from Herod's clutches and from everything the Jewish people were anticipating.'"

"When this had dawned on him, he went to the house of Mary the mother of John, also called Mark, **where many people had gathered and were praying.** Peter knocked at the outer entrance, and a servant girl named Rhoda came to answer the door. When she recognized Peter's voice, she was so overjoyed she ran back without opening it and exclaimed, 'Peter is at the door!'"

"'You're out of your mind,' they told her. When she kept insisting that it was so, they said, 'It must be his angel.' But Peter kept on knocking, and when they opened the door and saw him, they were astonished."

Acts 12:11-16

According to John Wesley's notes, he says it was a common opinion among the Jews that every man had his particular guardian angels, who frequently assumed both his shape and voice. This idea, however, is not found in any Scriptures. In the story only Rhoda had heard Peter's voice, and told the others. The people who said "it must be his angel" had not actually seen or heard Peter.

Daniel was rescued from the lion's den.

Daniel was a ruler in the land and because he had exceptional qualities, King Darius planned to set him over the whole kingdom. Some of the other rulers tried to find grounds against Daniel, but they couldn't find any faults in him. So they convinced the king that there should be a decree that anyone who worships any God or anyone except the king should be thrown in the lion's den. Daniel was caught bowing down and praying to God three times a day. As a result, he was thrown into the lion's den.

> "At the first light of dawn, the king got up and hurried to the lions' den. When he came near the den, he called to Daniel in an anguished voice, 'Daniel, servant of the living God, has your God, whom you serve continually, been able to rescue you from the lions?'"

> "Daniel answered, 'O king, live forever! My God sent His angel, and He shut the mouths of the lions. They have not hurt me, because I was found innocent in His sight. Nor have I ever done any wrong before you, O king.'"

> "The king was overjoyed and gave orders to lift Daniel out of the den. **And when Daniel was lifted from the den, no wound was found on him, because he had trusted in his God.**"

> Daniel 6:19-23

King Darius really liked Daniel and he didn't want to have him killed, but he had already signed a decree and had to go through with it. That's why it said "the king was overjoyed and gave orders to lift Daniel out of the den."

Notice in these next Scriptures it says as soon as Daniel began to pray, an answer was given.

> "While I was speaking and praying, confessing my sin and the sin of my people Israel and making my request to the Lord my God for His holy hill – while I was still in prayer, Gabriel, the man I had seen in the earlier vision, came to me in swift flight about the time of the evening sacrifice. He instructed me and said to me, 'Daniel, I have now come to give you insight and understanding. **As soon as you began to pray, an answer was given, which I have come to tell you, for you are highly esteemed.** Therefore, consider the message and understand the vision.'"
>
> Daniel 9:20-23

Paul and people in ship rescued.

Paul was in a ship when a great storm caused it to be shipwrecked. An angel appeared to Paul, and told him that he and all the people on this ship would survive.

> "Much time had been lost, and sailing had already become dangerous because by now it was after the Fast. So Paul warned them, 'Men, I can see that our voyage is going to be disastrous and bring great loss to ship and cargo, and to our own lives also.' But the centurion, instead of listening to what Paul said, followed the advice of the pilot and of the owner of the ship. Since the harbor was unsuitable to winter in, the majority decided that we should sail on, hoping to reach Phoenix

and winter there. This was a harbor in Crete, facing both southwest and northwest."

"When a gentle south wind began to blow, they thought they had obtained what they wanted; so they weighed anchor and sailed along the shore of Crete. Before very long, a wind of hurricane force, called the 'northeaster,' swept down from the island. The ship was caught by the storm and could not head into the wind; so we gave way to it and were driven along. As we passed to the lee of a small island called Cauda, we were hardly able to make the lifeboat secure. When the men had hoisted it aboard, they passed ropes under the ship itself to hold it together. Fearing that they would run aground on the sandbars of Syrtis, they lowered the sea anchor and let the ship be driven along. We took such a violent battering from the storm that the next day they began to throw the cargo overboard. On the third day, they threw the ship's tackle overboard with their own hands. When neither sun nor stars appeared for many days and the storm continued raging, we finally gave up all hope of being saved."

"After the men had gone a long time without food, Paul stood up before them and said: 'Men, you should have taken my advice not to sail from Crete; then you would have spared yourselves this damage and loss. But now I urge you to keep up your courage, because not one of you will be lost; only the ship will be destroyed. **Last night an angel of the God whose I am and whom I serve stood beside me and said, 'Do not be afraid, Paul. You must stand trial before Caesar; and God has graciously given you the lives of all who sail with you.'"**

Acts 27:9-24

Three men rescued from the fiery furnace.

This is an amazing story about three men who refused fall down and worship the image of gold as the king decreed. They trusted in God, were thrown into the fiery furnace, and God protected them all. He sent an angel into the fiery furnace with them!

"You have issued a decree, O king, that everyone who hears the sound of the horn, flute, zither, lyre, harp, pipes and all kinds of music must fall down and worship the image of gold, and that whoever does not fall down and worship will be thrown into a blazing furnace."

"But there are some Jews whom you have set over the affairs of the province of Babylon — Shadrach, Meshach and Abednego — who pay no attention to you, O king. They neither serve your gods nor worship the image of gold you have set up."

"Furious with rage, Nebuchadnezzar summoned Shadrach, Meshach and Abednego. So these men were brought before the king, and Nebuchadnezzar said to them, 'Is it true, Shadrach, Meshach and Abednego, that you do not serve my gods or worship the image of gold I have set up? Now when you hear the sound of the horn, flute, zither, lyre, harp, pipes and all kinds of music, if you are ready to fall down and worship the image I made, very good. But if you do not worship it, you will be thrown immediately into a blazing furnace. Then what god will be able to rescue you from my hand?'"

"Shadrach, Meshach and Abednego replied to the king, 'O Nebuchadnezzar, we do not need to defend ourselves before you in this matter. If we are thrown into the blazing furnace, the God we serve is able to save us from it, and He will rescue us from your hand, O king. But even if He does not, we want you to know,

O king, that we will not serve your gods or worship the image of gold you have set up.'"

"Then Nebuchadnezzar was furious with Shadrach, Meshach and Abednego, and his attitude toward them changed. He ordered the furnace heated seven times hotter than usual and commanded some of the strongest soldiers in his army to tie up Shadrach, Meshach and Abednego and throw them into the blazing furnace. So these men, wearing their robes, trousers, turbans and other clothes, were bound and thrown into the blazing furnace. The king's command was so urgent and the furnace so hot that the flames of the fire killed the soldiers who took up Shadrach, Meshach and Abednego, and these three men, firmly tied, fell into the blazing furnace. "

"Then King Nebuchadnezzar leaped to his feet in amazement and asked his advisers, 'Weren't there three men that we tied up and threw into the fire?' They replied, 'Certainly, O king.'"

"He said, 'Look! I see four men walking around in the fire, unbound and unharmed, and the fourth looks like a son of the gods.'"

"Nebuchadnezzar then approached the opening of the blazing furnace and shouted, 'Shadrach, Meshach and Abednego, servants of the Most High God, come out! Come here!' So Shadrach, Meshach and Abednego came out of the fire, and the satraps, prefects, governors and royal advisers crowded around them. They saw that the fire had not harmed their bodies, nor was a hair of their heads singed; their robes were not scorched, and there was no smell of fire on them."

"Then Nebuchadnezzar said, 'Praise be to the God of Shadrach, Meshach and Abednego, who has sent His angel and rescued His servants! They trusted in Him and defied the king's command and were willing to give up their lives rather than serve or worship any god except their own God. Therefore I decree that the people of any nation or language who say anything against the God of Shadrach, Meshach and Abednego be cut into pieces and their houses be turned into piles of rubble, for no other god can save in this way.'"

"Then the king promoted Shadrach, Meshach and Abednego in the province of Babylon."

Daniel 3:10-30

An Angel rescued the apostles.

An angel rescued the apostles from jail, and then he encouraged them to go out and tell all the people about the gospel of Jesus Christ.

"Then the high priest and all his associates, who were members of the party of the Sadducees, were filled with jealousy. They arrested the apostles and put them in the public jail. But during the night an angel of the Lord opened the doors of the jail and brought them out. 'Go, stand in the temple courts,' he said, 'and tell the people the full message of this new life.'"

Acts 5:17-20

Angels Sometimes Bring Food.

"Elijah was afraid and ran for his life. When he came to Beersheba in Judah, he left his servant there, while he himself went a day's journey into the desert. He came to a broom tree, sat down under it and prayed that he might die. 'I have had enough, Lord,' he said. 'Take my life; I am no better than my ancestors.' Then he lay down under the tree and fell asleep."

"All at once an angel touched him and said, 'Get up and eat.' He looked around, and there by his head was a cake of bread baked over hot coals, and a jar of water. He ate and drank and then lay down again."

"The angel of the Lord came back a second time and touched him and said, 'Get up and eat, for the journey is too much for you.' So he got up and ate and drank. Strengthened by that food, he traveled forty days and forty nights until he reached Horeb, the mountain of God. There he went into a cave and spent the night."

1 Kings 19:3-9

Here's another example of angels sending food to people.

"Yet He gave a command to the skies above and opened the doors of the heavens; he rained down manna for the people to eat, He gave them the grain of heaven. Men ate the bread of angels; He sent them all the food they could eat."

Psalm 78:23-25

We have learned that when we pray to God He often sends angels to assist us. We don't realize they are helping us most of the time, but they are. When we are blessed in a situation it isn't a coincidence, a matter of being in the right place at the right time or good luck. When we pray and live our lives for the Lord, we have angels that are assigned to watch over us and help us.

Chapter 6

Fallen Angels

Satan's rebellion and his fall, as well as the angels that went with him is definitely the down side to the study of angels. However, we need to look at this part of the picture in order to find out what happened. Lucifer was originally one of God's angels. He was a guardian cherub, and originally was full of wisdom and beauty.

One question that we don't find answered in the Bible is why Satan and the fallen angels were able to sin since they were created perfect and innocent. The only conclusion would be that, like Adam and Eve, and all of us, they were given a free will, and they made a very bad choice. In Ezekiel 28 it says that wickedness was found in Satan.

We do not understand why in God's wisdom He has allowed Satan and the fallen angels to continue with the powers that they have. The only conclusion seems to be that we all have a free will, and God wants us all to make our own choices. Also, I suppose that without witnessing the tragedy and pain of sin and evil, we would never know why it is important to avoid that path. We would not realize the destruction, pain, and suffering that would result in such actions. I know that if it was up to you or me, we would have said let's lock up Satan and the fallen angels, and be done with it right away. Let's not let them near mankind and let everything run smoothly. We just do not know or understand, but we have to have confidence that God has a good reason for this.

His name was Lucifer, frequently called Satan or the Devil.

There is certainly no loss for names to describe Lucifer, the fallen angel. Other references or names are "the dragon"

(Revelation 12:7), "King of Persia" (Daniel 10:13), "King of Tyre" (Ezekiel 28), and "the serpent" (Genesis 3). Check out the next verse that has four of his names in it.

> "This great **dragon** — the ancient **serpent** called the **Devil**, or **Satan**, the one deceiving the whole world — was thrown down to the earth with all his angels."
>
> Revelation 12:9

Jesus said that he was "the Prince of this world."

> "Now is the time for judgment on this world; now the prince of this world will be driven out."
>
> John 12:31

Another name for Satan is Beelzebub. We see this in these Scriptures.

> "Jesus was driving out a demon that was mute. When the demon left, the man who had been mute spoke, and the crowd was amazed. But some of them said, 'By Beelzebub the prince of demons, He is driving out demons.' Others tested Him by asking for a sign from heaven."

> "Jesus knew their thoughts and said to them: 'Any kingdom divided against itself will be ruined, and a house divided against itself will fall. If Satan is divided against himself, how can his kingdom stand? I say this because you claim that I drive out demons by Beelzebub. Now if I drive out demons by Beelzebub, by whom do your followers drive them out? So then, they will be your judges. But if I drive out demons by the finger of God, then the kingdom of God has come to you.'"
>
> Luke 11:14-20

The first time in Scripture that we hear about Lucifer is in the Garden of Eden when he convinced Eve to eat the forbidden fruit. You may be wondering how we know that the serpent was Satan. In Ezekiel 28 which we will read shortly, it states, "you were in Eden." We really don't know how long Adam and Eve lived in their perfect world in the Garden of Eden before they sinned. We do know that it was before they had children.

"Now the serpent was more crafty than any of the wild animals the Lord God had made. He said to the woman, did God really say, 'You must not eat from any tree in the garden'?"

"The woman said to the serpent, 'We may eat fruit from the trees in the garden, but God did say, You must not eat fruit from the tree that is in the middle of the garden, and you must not touch it, or you will die.'"

"'You will not surely die,' the serpent said to the woman. For God knows that when you eat of it your eyes will be opened, and you will be like God, knowing good and evil.'"

"When the woman saw that the fruit of the tree was good for food and pleasing to the eye, and also desirable for gaining wisdom, she took some and ate it. She also gave some to her husband, who was with her, and he ate it. Then the eyes of both of them were opened, and they realized they were naked; so they sewed fig leaves together and made coverings for themselves."

Genesis 3:1-7

I have often wondered what would have happened if Adam didn't eat the forbidden fruit after Eve had already eaten it, and instead said to her, "no thanks." I guess we'll never know how God would have handled the situation, but it's an interesting thought. I can tell you that through the following Scripture we know that Adam was not deceived. Perhaps he panicked because he didn't want to lose Eve, and foolishly decided to share her fate. Therefore, sin entered the world.

"And Adam was not the one deceived; it was the woman who was deceived and became a sinner."

1 Timothy 2:14

At another critical time in history the Devil was involved in more evil activities. In the next Scriptures we see that Satan possessed the body of Judas when he decided to betray Jesus.

"Jesus answered, 'It is the one to whom I will give this piece of bread when I have dipped it in the dish.' Then, dipping the piece of bread, He gave it to Judas Iscariot, son of Simon. As soon as Judas took the bread, Satan entered into him."

"'What you are about to do, do quickly,' Jesus told him, but no one at the meal understood why Jesus said this to him. Since Judas had charge of the money, some thought Jesus was telling him to buy what was needed for the Feast, or to give something to the poor. As soon as Judas had taken the bread, he went out."

John 13:26-30

Satan's personality traits.

He's a murderer and a liar.

"You belong to your father, the Devil, and you want to carry out your father's desire. He was a murderer from the beginning, not holding to the truth, for there is no truth in him. When he lies, he speaks his native language, for he is a liar and the father of lies."

John 8:44

He's a sinner.

"He who does what is sinful is of the Devil, because the Devil has been sinning from the beginning. The reason the Son of God appeared was to destroy the Devil's work."

> 1 John 3:8

He's an accuser.

> "Then I heard a loud voice in heaven say: 'Now have come the salvation and the power and the kingdom of our God, and the authority of His Christ. For the accuser of our brothers, who accuses them before our God day and night, has been hurled down."
>
> Revelation 12:10

He's our adversary.

> "Be sober, be vigilant; because your adversary the Devil, as a roaring lion, walketh about, seeking whom he may devour."
>
> 1 Peter 5:8

He's a deceiver who blinds the minds of people.

> "In whom the god of this world hath blinded the minds of them which believe not, lest the light of the glorious gospel of Christ, who is the image of God, should shine unto them."
>
> 2 Corinthians 4:4

What went wrong with Lucifer?

Satan fell as we see in this next verse. Then we'll look at what went wrong.

> I saw Satan fall like lightning from heaven.
>
> Luke 10:18

This Scripture talks about one of the reasons for his fall. It was his conceit and pride.

"He must not be a recent convert, or he may become conceited and fall under the same judgment as the Devil. He must also have a good reputation with outsiders, so that he will not fall into disgrace and into the Devil's trap."

1 Timothy 3:6-7

Other reasons for his fall were that he wanted to exalt his throne above the stars of God, and wanted to be like the most high. Basically, he was corrupted by personal ambition.

"How you have fallen from heaven, O morning star, son of the dawn! You have been cast down to the earth, you who once laid low the nations!"

"You said in your heart, 'I will ascend to heaven; I will raise my throne above the stars of God; I will sit enthroned on the mount of assembly, on the utmost heights of the sacred mountain.'"

"'I will ascend above the tops of the clouds; I will make myself like the Most High.' But you are brought down to the grave, to the depths of the pit."

Isaiah 14:12-15

There are a few things to notice about Satan's fall in the following Scriptures. I've put some important points in bold face so you can see them better. Satan was a guardian cherub. He had too much pride and said he was god, and he wanted to sit on the throne of god.

Another point is that these Scriptures state that Satan was in the Garden of Eden, which we know, but the way this is worded, it looks like he had not yet fallen when he first entered the Garden of Eden. It talks about him being in there, and being adorned with the precious stones at the time.

"The word of the Lord came to me: Son of man, say to the ruler of Tyre, This is what the Sovereign Lord says: **In the pride of your heart you say, 'I am a god; I sit** on the throne of a god in the heart of the seas.' But you are a man and not a god, though you think you are as wise as a god."

"Are you wiser than Daniel? Is no secret hidden from you? By your wisdom and understanding you have gained wealth for yourself and amassed gold and silver in your treasuries. By your great skill in trading you have increased your wealth, and because of your wealth your heart has grown proud."

"Therefore this is what the Sovereign Lord says: Because you think you are wise, as wise as a god, I am going to bring foreigners against you, the most ruthless of nations; they will draw their swords against your beauty and wisdom and pierce your shining splendor."

"They will bring you down to the pit, and you will die a violent death in the heart of the seas. Will you then say, 'I am a god,' in the presence of those who kill you? You will be but a man, not a god, in the hands of those who slay you. You will die the death of the uncircumcised at the hands of foreigners. I have spoken, declares the Sovereign Lord."

"The word of the Lord came to me: Son of man, take up a lament concerning the king of Tyre and say to him: 'This is what the Sovereign Lord says: You were the model of perfection, full of wisdom and perfect in beauty. **You were in Eden, the garden of God; every precious stone adorned you: ruby, topaz and emerald, chrysolite, onyx and jasper, sapphire, turquoise and beryl. Your settings and mountings were made of gold; on the day you were created they were prepared.**"

"You were anointed as **a guardian cherub**, for so I ordained you. You were on the holy mount of God; you walked among the fiery stones."

"You were blameless in your ways from the day you were created till wickedness was found in you. Through your widespread trade you were filled with violence, and you sinned. So I drove you in disgrace from the mount of God, and I expelled you, **O guardian cherub**, from among the fiery stones. **Your heart became proud on account of your beauty, and you corrupted your wisdom   because of your splendor.**   So I threw you to the earth; I made a spectacle of you before kings."

"By your many sins and dishonest trade you have desecrated your sanctuaries.   So I made a fire come out from you, and it consumed you, and I reduced you to ashes on the ground in the sight of all who were watching.   All the nations who knew you are appalled at you; you have come to a horrible end and will be no more."

> Ezekiel 28:1-19

Satan is declared the enemy of God and mankind.

"Be self-controlled and alert. Your enemy the Devil prowls around like a roaring lion looking for someone to devour."

> 1 Peter 5:8

"Put on the full armor of God so that you can take your stand against the Devil's schemes."

> Ephesians 6:11

The next verse tells us that when we sin we give the Devil a foothold or an entryway into our lives.

"'In your anger do not sin': 'Do not let the sun go down while you are still angry, and do not give the Devil a foothold.'"

Ephesians 4:26-27

"Be self-controlled and alert. Your enemy the Devil prowls around like a roaring lion looking for someone to devour."

1 Peter 5:8

In the next verse he is referred to as "the prince of the power of the air."

"Wherein in time past ye walked according to the course of this world, according to the prince of the power of the air, the spirit that now worketh in the children of disobedience."

Ephesians 2:2 (KJV)

He is referred to as "the god of this world," and he has power to blind the minds of unbelievers.

"The god of this age has blinded the minds of unbelievers, so that they cannot see the light of the gospel of the glory of Christ, who is the image of God."

2 Corinthians 4:4

Jesus was talking to the Apostle Paul at his conversion in the following verses. He said He wants people to turn from the power of Satan to God.

"'I am Jesus, whom you are persecuting,' the Lord replied. 'Now get up and stand on your feet. I have appeared to you to appoint you as a servant and as a witness of what you have seen of Me and what I will show you. I will rescue you from your own people and from the Gentiles. I am sending you to them to open their eyes and turn them from darkness to light, and from the power of Satan to God, so that they may

receive forgiveness of sins and a place among those
who are sanctified by faith in Me.'"

Acts 26:15-18

Jesus told the parable of the weeds.

First Jesus told the parable of the weeds, and then He explained
it.

"He told them still another parable: 'The kingdom of
heaven is like yeast that a woman took and mixed into a
large amount of flour until it worked all through the
dough.' Jesus spoke all these things to the crowd in
parables; He did not say anything to them without using
a parable. So was fulfilled what was spoken through
the prophet: I will open My mouth in parables, I will
utter things hidden since the creation of the world."

Matthew 13:33-35

The parable of the Weeds Explained.

"Then He left the crowd and went into the house. His
disciples came to Him and said, Explain to us the
parable of the weeds in the field. He answered, The
one who sowed the good seed is the Son of Man. The
field is the world, and the good seed stands for the sons
of the kingdom. The weeds are the sons of the evil one,
and the enemy who sows them is the Devil. The harvest
is the end of the age, and the harvesters are angels. As
the weeds are pulled up and burned in the fire, so it will
be at the end of the age."

Matthew 13:36-40

And we see that the Devil deceives the whole world.

"And the great dragon was cast out, that old serpent, called the Devil, and Satan, which deceiveth the whole world: he was cast out into the earth, and his angels were cast out with him."

"And I heard a loud voice saying in heaven, Now is come salvation, and strength, and the kingdom of our God, and the power of His Christ: for the accuser of our brethren is cast down, which accused them before our God day and night."

Revelation 12:9-10 (KJV)

About Demons.

Exactly who the demons, evil spirits, and unclean spirits are is a very perplexing question. It is the traditional view that they are fallen angels.

There are other theories about who demons are, but I do not see sufficient evidence in the Bible to prove them out. They apparently are devoid of a body of their own, because they seem to be looking for bodies to possess as you'll see in some of these Scriptures. One thing is sure, and that is that they are of the Devil, and take orders from him.

Some people don't think the fallen angels can be demons because the fallen angels don't seek to inhabit any beings. However, this is not true since Satan possessed Judas (John 13:26-30) as well as the serpent in the Garden of Eden.

We know a little bit about these demons. They know there is only one God. Why they have followed Satan when they know he cannot replace God is a mystery. Perhaps it's a misery loves company mindset.

"You believe that there is one God. Good! Even the demons believe that — and shudder."

James 2:19

They tout a false doctrine with deceiving spirits.

> "The Spirit clearly says that in later times some will abandon the faith and follow deceiving spirits and things taught by demons. Such teachings come through hypocritical liars, whose consciences have been seared as with a hot iron."
>
> 1 Timothy 4:1-2

Evil Spirits.

There are various spirits mentioned in the Bible. Here are some of them.

Spirit Of Infirmity

According to the Bible there are many causes for sickness. In this case it was caused by a spirit of infirmity.

> "And, behold, there was a woman which had a spirit of infirmity eighteen years, and was bowed together, and could in no wise lift up herself."
>
> "And when Jesus saw her, He called her to Him, and said unto her, Woman, thou art loosed from thine infirmity."
>
> "And He laid His hands on her: and immediately she was made straight, and glorified God."
>
> Luke 13:11-13 (KJV)

Lying Spirit

Evidently, there is a "lying spirit."

> "And there came forth a spirit, and stood before the Lord, and said, I will persuade him. And the Lord said unto him, Wherewith? And he said, I will go forth, and I will be a lying spirit in the mouth of all his prophets.

And he said, Thou shalt persuade him, and prevail also: go forth, and do so."

1 Kings 22:21-22 (KJV)

Spirit of Bondage

"For ye have not received the spirit of bondage again to fear; but ye have received the Spirit of adoption, whereby we cry, Abba, Father."

Romans 8:15 (KJV)

Spirit of Divination

"And it came to pass, as we went to prayer, a certain damsel possessed with a spirit of divination met us, which brought her masters much gain by soothsaying."

Acts 16:16 (KJV)

They know exactly who Jesus is, and they know He can cast them out of a person.

"Just then a man in their synagogue who was possessed by an evil spirit cried out, 'What do you want with us, Jesus of Nazareth? Have you come to destroy us? I know who you are — the Holy One of God!'"

"'Be quiet!' said Jesus sternly. 'Come out of him!' The evil spirit shook the man violently and came out of him with a shriek."

Mark 1:23-26

They also know that their ultimate fate is to be tortured in hell.

"'What do you want with us, Son of God?' they shouted. 'Have You come here to torture us before the appointed time?'"

Matthew 8:29

As we have seen, people can be demon possessed.

"When evening came, many who were demon-
possessed were brought to Him, and He drove out the
spirits with a word and healed all the sick."

Matthew 8:16

Demons can possess animals, but only appeared to be able to
do so with special permission by Jesus.

"When He arrived at the other side in the region of the
Gadarenes, two demon-possessed men coming from the
tombs met Him. They were so violent that no one
could pass that way. 'What do you want with us, Son of
God?' they shouted. 'Have you come here to torture us
before the appointed time?'"

"Some distance from them a large herd of pigs was
feeding. The demons begged Jesus, 'If you drive us out,
send us into the herd of pigs.'"

"He said to them, 'Go!' So they came out and went into
the pigs, and the whole herd rushed down the steep
bank into the lake and died in the water. Those tending
the pigs ran off, went into the town and reported all
this, including what had happened to the demon-
possessed men. Then the whole town went out to meet
Jesus. And when they saw Him, they pleaded with Him
to leave their region."

Matthew 8:28-35

Can Christians be demon possessed? No. Take a look at these
verses. They state that we are not unoccupied, but we are
occupied with the Holy Spirit.

"When an evil spirit comes out of a man, it goes
through arid places seeking rest and does not find it.
Then it says, 'I will return to the house I left.' When it
arrives, it finds the house unoccupied, swept clean and
put in order. Then it goes and takes with it seven other
spirits more wicked than itself, and they go in and live

there. And the final condition of that man is worse than the first. That is how it will be with this wicked generation."

Matthew 12:43-45

Here we see the Apostle Paul says that when we are born again, God puts His seal of ownership on us.

"For no matter how many promises God has made, they are 'Yes' in Christ. And so through Him the 'Amen' is spoken by us to the glory of God. Now it is God who makes both us and you stand firm in Christ. He anointed us, set His seal of ownership on us, and put His Spirit in our hearts as a deposit, guaranteeing what is to come.

2 Corinthians 1:20-22

We are the temple of the Holy Spirit.

"Do you not know that your body is a temple of the Holy Spirit, who is in you, whom you have received from God? You are not your own."

1 Corinthians 6:19

So the enemy can attack us, but as born again believer's we cannot be demon possessed.

Getting rid of the Devil.

In these Scriptures we receive council on how to stop harassment from the Devil. The Bible doesn't say we won't have trouble or that the Devil won't try, but rather it instructs us on how to overcome the attacks of the Devil. Resisting the Devil will make him flee from you.

"Submit yourselves, then, to God. Resist the Devil, and he will flee from you."

James 4:7

There are some key things in the next verses to help us fight against the Devil. We have to be grounded in the truth from the Word of God, live a righteous life, have the gospel of peace, keep the faith, have the helmet of salvation, and always keep praying.

"Finally, be strong in the Lord and in His mighty power. Put on the full armor of God so that you can take your stand against the Devil's schemes. For our struggle is not against flesh and blood, but against the rulers, against the authorities, against the powers of this dark world and against the spiritual forces of evil in the heavenly realms. Therefore put on the full armor of God, so that when the day of evil comes, you may be able to stand your ground, and after you have done everything, to stand. Stand firm then, with the belt of truth buckled around your waist, with the breastplate of righteousness in place, and with your feet fitted with the readiness that comes from the gospel of peace."

"In addition to all this, take up the shield of faith, with which you can extinguish all the flaming arrows of the evil one. Take the helmet of salvation and the sword of the Spirit, which is the word of God. And pray in the Spirit on all occasions with all kinds of prayers and requests. With this in mind, be alert and always keep on praying for all the saints."

Ephesians 6:10-18

In these verses I think David expresses how we can sometimes feel, and we can relate to him.

"Contend, O Lord, with those who contend with me; fight against those who fight against me. Take up shield and buckler; arise and come to my aid. Brandish spear and javelin against those who pursue me. Say to my soul, 'I am your salvation.' May those who seek my life be disgraced and put to shame; may those who plot my ruin be turned back in dismay. May they be like

chaff before the wind, with the angel of the Lord
driving them away; may their path be dark and slippery,
with the angel of the Lord pursuing them. Since they
hid their net for me without cause and without cause
dug a pit for me."

Psalm 35:1-7

It was through the word of God that Jesus defeated the Devil in
the wilderness. That's how He got the Devil to leave. He
insisted and persisted by quoting the word of God, and He
pushed back at the Devil until he gave up. This is one reason
why it's important to acquaint ourselves with the Scriptures. In
that way we will be able to defeat the enemy, and be victorious
as Jesus was in the following story. Another point to make is
how well Satan knows the Scriptures. Notice how easily he
continues to quote them while distorting the meaning of them.

"Then Jesus was led by the Spirit into the desert to be
tempted by the Devil. After fasting forty days and forty
nights, he was hungry. The tempter came to Him and
said, 'If you are the Son of God, tell these stones to
become bread.' Jesus answered, It is written: 'Man does
not live on bread alone, but on every word that comes
from the mouth of God.'"

"Then the Devil took Him to the holy city and had Him
stand on the highest point of the temple. 'If you are the
Son of God,' he said, 'throw yourself down. For it is
written: He will command His angels concerning you,
and they will lift you up in their hands, so that you will
not strike your foot against a stone. Jesus answered
him, It is also written: 'Do not put the Lord your God
to the test.' Again, the Devil took Him to a very high
mountain and showed Him all the kingdoms of the
world and their splendor. 'All this I will give you,' he
said, 'if you will bow down and worship me.' Jesus
said to him, 'Away from Me, Satan! For it is written:

'Worship the Lord your God, and serve Him only.'
Then the Devil left Him, and angels came and attended
Him."

Matthew 4:1-11

Each time the Devil tried to tempt Jesus, He quoted the
Scriptures. Finally, the Devil left Him, and the angels came to
attend to Him. This is why we need to keep quoting the
Scriptures all the time, and especially when we are in need.
For example, if we're sick we quote "By His stripes we are
healed," and if we need something we quote "God will supply
all my needs according to His riches in glory."

Encouragement through the Scriptures.

I realize that reading about Satan, the fallen angels, and demon
spirits is a bit depressing, therefore, I hope the following
Scriptures will bring you comfort to know that the Lord is
helping us.

"I have told you these things, so that in Me you may
have peace. In this world you will have trouble. But
take heart! I have overcome the world."

John 16:33

"No weapon forged against you will prevail, and you
will refute every tongue that accuses you. This is the
heritage of the servants of the Lord, and this is their
vindication from Me, 'declares the Lord.'"

Isaiah 54:17

"A righteous man may have many troubles, but the
Lord delivers him from them all."

Psalm 34:19

"The Lord is a refuge for the oppressed, a stronghold in
times of trouble. 'Those who know Your name will

trust in You, for You, Lord, have never forsaken those who seek You.'"

Psalm 9:9-10

"He will call upon Me, and I will answer Him; I will be with him in trouble, I will deliver him and honor him."

Psalm 91:15

"Wait for the Lord; be strong and take heart and wait for the Lord."

Psalm 27:14

"In the morning, O Lord, you hear my voice; in the morning I lay my requests before you and wait in expectation."

Psalm 5:3

"For in the day of trouble He will keep me safe in His dwelling; He will hide me in the shelter of His tabernacle and set me high upon a rock."

Psalm 27:5

"You are my hiding place; You will protect me from trouble and surround me with songs of deliverance."

Psalm 32:7

"But I call to God, and the Lord saves me. Evening, morning and noon I cry out in distress, and He hears my voice."

Psalm 55:16-17

"I lift up my eyes to the hills — where does my help come from? My help comes from the Lord, the Maker of heaven and earth."

Psalm 121:1-2

"...If God is for us, who can be against us?"

Romans 8:31 (KJV)

"... then the Lord knows how to rescue godly men from trials and to hold the unrighteous for the day of judgment, while continuing their punishment."

2 Peter 2:9

"Come to Me, all you who are weary and burdened, and I will give you rest."

Matthew 11:28

And, finally, let's look at this Scripture which tells us that angels are stronger and more powerful than the Devil and his fallen angels. That means we have the best and the strongest team working for us!

"Bold and arrogant, these men are not afraid to slander celestial beings; yet even angels, although they are stronger and more powerful, do not bring slanderous accusations against such beings in the presence of the Lord."

2 Peter 2:11

I would recommend Hebrews Chapter 11 to read for encouragement and faith. There we find so many references to the people in the Old Testament who had faith in God. In Romans 15:4 it says "For everything that was written in the past was written to teach us, so that through endurance and the encouragement of the Scriptures we might have hope." The following chapters are also very comforting and supportive: Psalm 23, 30, 31, 91, 103, and John 14.

The Devil can display counterfeit miracles.

We may have wondered how or why there are some miracles that followers of Satan can perform. Apparently Satan has the ability to imitate or mimic miracles, and these would be performed by followers of Satan.

> "The coming of the lawless one will be in accordance with the work of Satan displayed in all kinds of counterfeit miracles, signs and wonders."
>
> 2 Thessalonians 2:9

One-third of the angels fell with Satan.

It is widely believed by Bible scholars that one-third of the angels fell with Satan. This next verse seems to be where this belief originates.

> "His tail swept a third of the stars out of the sky and flung them to the earth. The dragon stood in front of the woman who was about to give birth, so that he might devour her child the moment it was born."
>
> Revelation 12:4

Whether it was one-third of the angels or not may be up for debate, but you can see by this next verse that Satan definitely took some of the angels with him.

> "The great dragon was hurled down — that ancient serpent called the Devil, or Satan, who leads the whole world astray. He was hurled to the earth, and his angels with him."
>
> Revelation 12:9

Satan has access to God.

Satan still appears to have access to God, but it's restricted. In these Scriptures God is conversing with Satan, and He said "Have you considered my servant Job?"

"One day the angels came to present themselves before the Lord, and Satan also came with them. The Lord said to Satan, 'Where have you come from?' Satan answered the Lord, 'From roaming through the earth and going back and forth in it.'"

"Then the Lord said to Satan, 'Have you considered my servant Job? There is no one on earth like him; he is blameless and upright, a man who fears God and shuns evil.'"

"'Does Job fear God for nothing?' Satan replied. 'Have you not put a hedge around him and his household and everything he has? You have blessed the work of his hands, so that his flocks and herds are spread throughout the land. But stretch out your hand and strike everything he has, and he will surely curse You to Your face.'"

"The Lord said to Satan, 'Very well, then, everything he has is in your hands, but on the man himself do not lay a finger.' Then Satan went out from the presence of the Lord."

Job 1:6-12

"On another day the angels came to present themselves before the Lord, and Satan also came with them to present himself before Him."

Job 2:1

Another reference to his access to God is in this Scripture where it states "against the spiritual forces of evil in the heavenly realms." We can see by this statement that spiritual forces or Satan and his fallen angels have some access to heavenly realms.

"For our struggle is not against flesh and blood, but against the rulers, against the authorities, against the powers of this dark world and against the spiritual forces of evil in the heavenly realms."

Ephesians 6:12

For more references to Satan's access to God, please see Revelation 12:10 and Zechariah 3:1-2 in the next section.

Satan accuses God's people.

In these verses we can see that Satan apparently accuses God's people of sin or at least he tries to. Again, we see that he still has access to God, and he accuses us day and night.

"Then I heard a loud voice in heaven say: 'Now have come the salvation and the power and the kingdom of our God, and the authority of His Christ. For the accuser of our brothers, who accuses them before our God day and night, has been hurled down.'"

Revelation 12:10

"Then he showed me Joshua the high priest standing before the angel of the Lord, and Satan standing at his right side to accuse him. The Lord said to Satan, 'The Lord rebuke you, Satan! The Lord, who has chosen Jerusalem, rebuke you! Is not this man a burning stick snatched from the fire?''

Zechariah 3:1-2

What is the final destiny of Lucifer and the fallen angels?

In these Scriptures we see a clear picture of what is in store for Satan and the fallen angels. Ultimately, they're getting a one-way ticket to hell where they will enjoy eternal fire, and will be tormented day and night forever and ever. The ironic thing about that is that they know this is what is going to happen, but they still persist in their destructive course.   In the next Scripture two men who were possessed by demons ask Jesus what He wants with them. They want to know if He has come to torture them before the appointed time!

"When He arrived at the other side in the region of the Gadarenes, two demon-possessed men coming from the tombs met Him.   They were so violent that no one could pass that way. 'What do You want with us, Son of God?' they shouted. 'Have you come here to torture us before the appointed time?'"

Matthew 8:28-29

Here are some other verses that tell us about their destiny.

"Then He will say to those on His left, 'Depart from Me, you who are cursed, into the eternal fire prepared for the Devil and his angels.'"

Matthew 25:41

"And the Devil, who deceived them, was thrown into the lake of burning sulfur, where the beast and the false prophet had been thrown. They will be tormented day and night for ever and ever."

Revelation 20:10

"How art thou fallen from heaven, O Lucifer, son of the morning! How art thou cut down to the ground, which didst weaken the nations! For thou hast said in thine heart, I will ascend into heaven, I will exalt my throne above the stars of God: I will sit also upon the mount of the congregation, in the sides of the north: 'I will ascend above the heights of the clouds; I will be like the most High. Yet thou shalt be brought down to hell, to the sides of the pit.'"

Isaiah 14:12-15 (KJV)

"For if God did not spare angels when they sinned, but sent them to hell, putting them into gloomy dungeons to be held for judgment ..."

2 Peter 2:4

Some fallen angels are locked up.

Some of Satan's fallen angels have been reserved in chains until judgment day. Also, see 2 Peter 2:4 above.

"And the angels who did not keep their positions of authority but abandoned their own home — these He has kept in darkness, bound with everlasting chains for judgment on the great Day."

Jude 1:6

Some fallen angels are free.

The remainder of the fallen angels are free, and are thought to be demons or devils to whom reference is constantly made throughout the New Testament.

"When he saw Jesus from a distance, he ran and fell on his knees in front of him. He shouted at the top of his voice, 'What do you want with me, Jesus, Son of the Most High God? Swear to God that you won't torture me!' For Jesus had said to him, 'Come out of this man, you evil spirit!'"

"Then Jesus asked him, 'What is your name?' 'My name is Legion,' he replied, 'for we are many.' And he begged Jesus again and again not to send them out of the area."

Mark 5:6-10

"The Spirit clearly says that in later times some will abandon the faith and follow deceiving spirits and things taught by demons."

1 Timothy 4:1

Fallen Angels Versus Fallen Man.

It should be noted that there is a difference in the fall of the Devil and the fallen angels and the fall of man. What I am referring to is that when man fell, everyone in the race fell. On the other hand, when the angels fell, only those individuals that sinned fell.

The fall of man.

When we consider the relationship between members of the human race, we realize we are all from one common origin and ancestry. We are all related or descendent from each other. The whole human race is descended from a single pair, one man and woman – Adam and Eve. Satan was in the form of a serpent in the Garden of Eden, and induced Eve to sin. When Adam and Eve fell, the race altogether fell, and therefore, the fate of all individuals was bound together. The root of mankind was perverted. They did not have any children until after they sinned, therefore, all men and women are born in sin.

We all share in a bloodline from our original parents. There is a great significance in our blood. The Bible says that the soul is in the blood. Here is one of the Scriptures that talks about the soul being in the blood.

"For the life of the flesh is in the blood: and I have given it to you upon the altar to make an atonement for your souls: for it is the blood that maketh an atonement for the soul."

Leviticus 17:11 (KJV)

This is the reason why it was necessary for Christ to die on the cross for our sins. Because without the shedding of blood there is no remission of sins. Through one man's disobedience we were all made sinners. And we know that through Jesus Christ those who are born again are restored to fellowship with God.

> "For just as through the disobedience of the one man the many were made sinners, so also through the obedience of the one man the many will be made righteous."
>
> Romans 5:19

The fall of the angels.

The angels are a collection of individuals that are often referred to in the Bible as a host, a company, or an army. There is no inference that there is any bloodline connection between them. And because of this they are responsible only for themselves. So when some angels fell, it apparently did not affect the other angels. Because the angels are a company and not a race they sinned individually, and not in some head of a race.

Angels are a Company as stated in the next verse. They are not a race as we are.

> "But ye are come unto mount Sion, and unto the city of the living God, the heavenly Jerusalem, and to an innumerable company of angels."
>
> Hebrews 12:22 (KJV)

The angels had a free will just as man does, which means that they have the ability to sin as well as the ability not to sin. We, therefore, have to conclude that the fall of the angels was due to deliberate revolt against God. Therefore, they lost their original holiness, and became corrupt in nature and conduct. So only those angels that decided to follow Satan were lost and separated from God.

In this chapter we have learned about the fallen angels, including Lucifer. We know that they are our enemy as well as God's enemy. We learned that Satan still has access to God, and that as many as one-third of the angels fell with him.

Chapter 7

Stories Of Angel Encounters

Angels take a women to heaven in a near-death situation.

A book written by Dr. Sabom called *Light & Death* tells many interesting stories of the study of Christian people who have had near-death experiences. The following is a summary of the story of a woman who was hospitalized with a ruptured tubal pregnancy, and a massive abdominal infection.

The woman said that two angels came down to get her. They never spoke to her, but each one took her by the hand and they were going up. As they went up she was looking back, and could see the doctors working on her.

She said, "please, take me back, I have my children to raise." However, they ignored her. As they got closer, it got brighter, and there was wonderful music she could hear.

When they got to the top she saw the Lord. She said she asked if she could go back and He said, "take her back."

She said the light was beautiful, and it was bright all around the Lord. His voice was commanding yet gentle.

When the Lord said, "take her back," she was turned around, and the descent was so rapid, it seemed to be 10 times faster than when going up.

When she got back to earth and into her body she didn't wake up for three days. When she finally woke up, the doctor said, "we thought we lost you."

Angels apear to a minister.

Roland Buck was a minister who had many visitations from angels, and these encounters are recorded in a book called

Angels On Assignment by Charles and Frances Hunter. If you have a chance to get this book, it is really interesting.

On one occasion, Pastor Buck said that he was halfway down the stairs when the light flipped on. Standing in front of him were two of the largest men he had ever seen in his life. He was shocked. He wasn't frightened, but there was such a radiation of divine power and brightness of God's presence that he couldn't stand up. His knees buckled, and he started to fall. One of the angels reached out and took hold of him.

The angel told him that his name was Gabriel. He was stunned, thinking could this be the same Gabriel that he read about in the Bible? He introduced the other angel to him and said his name of Chrioni.

The angel told Pastor Buck that seeing what was happening throughout the whole earth, he detected a massive build-up of satanic forces who were planning to attack him. The Spirit not only monitors, but sends out orders, so at God's command, the angels were sent to Boise, Idaho to defeat the enemy!

Chinese children that had visions and went to heaven.

There's an interesting book called *Visions Of Heaven* by H. A. Baker. The many experiences that these Chinese children had in heaven are documented in the book. Here is a little of what they saw.

The children from Adullam school entered heaven by its pearly gates into the city of golden streets. There were angels everywhere. They said, "Angels, angels everywhere. Angels talking, angels singing, angels rejoicing, angels playing harps and blowing trumpets, angels dancing and praising the King." They said this was a city of joy, where there was no more death, no sorrow. There was joy unspeakable and full of glory!

My friend, Shirley, has had a few encounters with angels. She would like to share these two with us.

An angel visited Shirley.

"I had been having some physical problems, severe pain in my stomach for days, and did not know what was happening. I prayed and asked the Lord to help me."

"That night I awoken and there was a light in my room. I turned towards the light and lo and behold there stood a large, and I mean large, angel dressed in a blue long dress, and she had wings. In front of her stood what appeared to be a little boy, but could have been a smaller angel, I am not sure since the presence of the larger angel filled half of my bedroom wall. They were merely looking at me and smiling."

"They stayed there smiling for several minutes, and all I could do was lay there and look at them. Then they simply faded from sight."

"I soon learned that I had a kidney stone, and if anyone has ever experienced that they know the pain it can bring. I truly feel the Lord sent His angels to strengthen me for what I was to go through the next few weeks. To this day the memory thrills me, and brings me great peace and joy."

An angel sang with Shirley and her nephew.

"I was singing with my nephew, Michael. We have received many, many songs from the Lord."

"Anyway, one day while in prayer I heard the Lord speak to me to get Michael and go to the church ... to begin singing praises to Him on a certain note, and that a special song would be born."

"We did that and almost immediately I heard the song, and started to sing it. We were recording, as we always did since we would not remember the song afterwards if we did not."

"As we sang we began to experience the Spirit of the Lord. It kept getting stronger and stronger and within seconds we started to hear other voices singing with us. We knew not to stop singing but to continue on, as we did, we kept on experiencing great heights in the Spirit of God."

"When we were finished we sat dazed for several minutes, not even able to talk."

"As soon as we could we listened to the tape, and unbelievably we could hear a voice singing with us. Clear as a bell."

"I sing second soprano, this voice was high, first soprano, and you can hear her singing each word distinctly with us. We were thrilled. After that we heard men's voices and women's voices from time to time during our worship sessions, but never again was the experience so sweet."

"A friend from New York City took the CD, and had it tested. They showed that there were definitely three voices singing on it. I still listen to this song over and over again, and never tire of hearing the voice of an angel singing praises to our King. It was a true blessing from God, an honor as far as I am concerned."

An angel helped a minister.

I heard one minister tell the story of how in his early days in the ministry he didn't have much money, and his car wasn't in very good shape. He was traveling with his wife in his car when it broke down. A man drove by and stopped to see if he could help him. He needed have the car towed to a repair shop. The stranger said he would come back with a truck to tow him to a station. This was back in the days before cell phones so having this person stop by was a real blessing. Today you could just call AAA or some local repair shop. He came back in a little while, and towed him to the shop. The stranger opened the repair shop, repaired the minister's car, and didn't take any money.

A couple of months later the minister was driving through the same town, and decided to stop to thank the owner of the repair shop. When he got there the shop was closed so the minister went across the street to a diner to inquire about it. The owner of the diner said that the repair shop had been closed for 10 years! He replied that someone had repaired his car in that service station. The man from the diner said that there hasn't been any power on in that repair shop for 10 years, and it's been closed all those years! At that point the minister knew that the stranger that had helped him was an angel sent by God.

Angels Protected Niki's Dad.

My father told us a story many years ago about how he and another minister were on their way to a church service. They got lost and pulled over to use a public telephone (this was long before cell phones were invented). The neighborhood was rough and there were several people around that looked threatening. They prayed quickly to themselves for God's protection.

While my Dad and the other man were at the phone, a couple of big, ominous looking men came up to them as if they would start trouble. My Dad said it was the most amazing thing, because these men looked at my Dad, they looked at his friend, and then they looked beside them and up a little higher as though they saw other men with them that were much bigger than my Dad, who was 6 feet tall. Immediately, they turned around and left.

My Dad is convinced that there were angels standing there protecting them. My Dad and his friend couldn't see the angels. But God gave these other men the ability to see into the spiritual world. They saw these angels standing there, who appeared as men who were stronger than they, and it put fear into their hearts. There are scores of stories about how angelic beings have come to the rescue of people, and most assuredly, there are incidences where angels have helped us, and we haven't even had a clue that they did so.

A very special white cat or an angel disguised as a cat?

I've told this story before, but I think it bears repeating in our discussion of angels. Whether this was an angel disguised as a cat or a cat from Heaven, I don't know. I think it could have been either.

Fourteen wonderful years with Pete, our cat, had passed since we adopted him at age 8. It was a couple of weeks before Pete passed away that he was sitting on the bay window in the dining room. I went over to see him, and there I saw a beautiful pure white cat outside directly in front of the window where he sat. The white cat was staring up at Pete. I called Jack, to come over to see this white cat that seemed to be in a trance as she gazed up at Pete. Jack came over to take a look, and within a couple of minutes she vanished from sight. I immediately ran outside to leave her some food in case she came back, but all the while I had an uneasy feeling inside me that this was no ordinary cat. There are very few outdoor cats in our neighborhood; we never saw this white cat before, and we've never seen her since. I couldn't get it out of my mind that the beautiful feline was a heavenly being, or an angel in the appearance of a cat, ready to take Pete to heaven.

I asked Jack if we could pray for Pete a little later that night. We had prayed for him constantly, often anointing him with oil. We prayed that night and I claimed the Word of God. Jack said, "That was one powerful prayer." I was giving it my all, because I was very concerned that the Lord was trying to show us something – that it was time for Pete to go home. Within a couple of weeks Pete did pass away from a heart attack.

Pete lived to be 21, close to 22 years old, which is a generous lifespan for a cat – not enough when you love someone – but generous in terms of a cat's lifespan. He enjoyed a very loving life with us, and was really only sick the last year of his life. He had urinary tract problems, which were under control, but toward his last years he developed kidney and heart disease. I believe that our prayers and trust in God gave him a longer life than he would ordinarily have had. Even though it pains us deeply to have him go, we know he's with the Lord and waiting for us to join him someday in heaven.

A sick child has an angelic visit.

In a *New York Times* article dated November 17, 1886, there was a story about a girl named Nora Brown in Owensborough, Kentucky. While she was suffering with a fever there was quite a stir in the family circle when she suddenly exclaimed that she saw an angel. She said the messenger told her in clear tones, "Thou shalt live another year." She further said that she felt his hands on her knees. The article said she was not given to exaggeration, and it was certainly a strange message.

While I don't like to leave you with a cliffhanger, I was unable to find out what happened to little Nora Brown. I made some telephone calls only to find out that the death records for this county in Kentucky only go back as far as 1911. Like you, I wanted to know if she died a year later.

Miracle involving an angel.

A *Fox News* story dated December 24, 2008 told about a severely ill teenager in North Carolina. Colleen, the girl's mother, said that an angel saved the life of her dying daughter. She actually took a picture of what appeared to be an angel. Chelsea was suffering from an advanced case of pneumonia in November – the latest in a string of illnesses in her short lifetime. Her mother said, "We had been praying every day, my oldest daughter and I and Chelsea." We were "praying for a miracle."

The pneumonia spread from her left lung to her right lung. Then she had sepsis and blood clots, staph infections, E. coli, a collapsed lung, and feeding problems. In October doctors wondered whether to take Chelsea off the ventilator. They tried several times before, but each time, Chelsea struggled to breathe. Finally, the family and doctors decided to take her off the ventilator. At first she did well, but the next day her health started to falter. She began having anxiety attacks with the oxygen mask over her face. As family and friends went to visit Chelsea – for what they thought was the last time – and prayed over what to do – a nurse practitioner called Colleen's attention to a nearby monitor, which displayed the door to the pediatric intensive care unit.

"On the monitor, there was this bright light," Colleen said. "And I looked at it, and said, Oh, my goodness! It looks like an angel." She immediately took out her camera and captured the image. This picture can still be viewed on the Fox News website. Three days later Chelsea went home, and her family believes that a miracle had occurred.

Angels rescue a women.

A *Newsweek Magazine* article dated December 27, 1993, entitled *Angels* told a story about Chantal. She and her fiancé, Dale, were exploring the Oregon coast when he lost his footing. As Dale plummeted to his death, Chantal shouted, "Please God! Help Me!" and was immediately surrounded by a cloud of angels 400 feet above the sea. She said, "It was like whiteness all around," and recalls that she could almost hear singing. Steadied by the heavenly host, she managed to climb down the otherwise impassable cliff.

Healing miracle and visiting angel.

A *Time Magazine* article dated December 27, 1993 called *Angels Among Us* included a story about a lady named Ann who was dying of cancer. One morning three days before surgery her husband answered the doorbell. Standing on the step was a large man, a good inch taller than her 6 foot 5 inch husband. He was a black man and had deep, deep azure blue eyes. The stranger introduced himself as Thomas. And then he told her that her cancer was gone.

Thomas came inside and told them they could stop worrying. He quoted Scripture to them – Isaiah 53:5 " ... and with His stripes we are healed. Ann still confused, looked at the man and demanded, "Who are you?" He said, "I am Thomas. I am sent by God."

Next, Ann recalls he held up his right hand, his palm was facing her, and he leaned toward her. There was heat coming from his hand. Suddenly her legs went out from under her and she fell to the floor. As she lay there, a strong white light traveled through her body. Meanwhile Thomas disappeared. She got up and knew something supernatural had happened.

She told the doctor she was healed, and didn't need the surgery. The doctor, being doubtful of this miracle, made a compromise and said to show up at the hospital as scheduled and they would do another biopsy before the surgery. At her bedside the doctor said he didn't know what happened, but her test came back clean. She said even her doctor said that they'd witnessed a medical miracle!

Angel Warriors During WWI.

A *New York Times* article dated October 17, 1915 revealed an interesting story. In one particular conflict referred to as "The Battle of Mons" it seems that there were some strange happenings told by both English and French soldiers. There were numerous soldiers that gave testimony of seeing angels. It was reported that the failure of Germans to capture Paris had been attributed to various causes, but never properly explained.

They say that on or about August 28, 1914 around eight in the evening soldiers started to ask each other if they saw anything startling. They said they saw a strange light which seemed to be distinctly outlined, and was not a reflection of the moon, nor were there any clouds. The light became brighter and they could see three shapes, one in the center looked to have outspread wings, the other two were not as large. They appeared to have long, loose-hanging garments of a golden tint, and they were above the German line facing them.

Perhaps we will never know exactly what happened, but with so many soldiers all witnessing the same thing, it seems apparent that these soldiers had some angelic help that day.

An amazing near-death experience.

As a result of a car collision, Dorothy had a near-death experience. She found herself suspended over the scene of the accident, viewing her limp and bleeding body held lifeless between the steering wheel and the driver's seat. Suddenly and instantly she said she was aware of what the drivers in the cars lined up behind her smashed vehicle were saying. They said things like, "Damn, this is just what I need – a car crash," and "I wonder how long I'm going to be stuck here."

Then Dorothy said she noticed a bright illuminated beam of light shooting out of the fifth car stuck behind her crashed automobile. As soon as she wondered what the beam of light was she said she found herself next to the woman in that car, who had instantly gone into prayer for her. And then Dorothy became aware that the beam of light that was flowing directly from this woman upward toward the heavens seemed to cause another beam of light to flow directly down into her. She wondered who this woman was, and instantly she noticed the license plate number of the woman's car and memorized it.

Then Dorothy heard an angelic voice calling to her. The angel was instructing her to return to her body, because the time was not yet right for her to return home. She was still required to remain on the earth.

She said it took her months to recover from the accident, but when she did she tracked down the woman through that license plate number. She went to her home with a bouquet of flowers to thank her for praying for her on that night when her body lay shattered. Imagine the surprise and amazement this woman must have experienced when Dorothy showed up to tell her the story of how her prayers impacted her life.

I thought this story was absolutely amazing! Imagine being in a near-death experience during an accident, and then being able to see what the people are saying and doing in the cars right behind you. Thank God for this lovely woman who prayed for her, and made the difference between life and death. Think of the visual image of seeing beams of light going from the praying woman into heaven, and then seeing them beam down onto yourself. It definitely makes our prayers more meaningful and significant.

A vital point to consider is how important it is for us as Christians to pray for people who are apparently in trouble even though we don't know who they are. We should all pray when we hear sirens and see car accidents, ambulances, fires, or other tragedies whether they are around us or we see them in the news. We can all let our lights shine up to heaven, and then beam back down to people in need. Who knows, maybe someday someone will show up at our door with a bouquet of flowers to thank us!

We have read of many fascinating stories about how angels help people every day. Although most of us do not have a dramatic story to share, we know that God has angels that are assigned to watch over us, and bless us in many ways.

Someday in heaven I believe the Lord will share with us all the many stories in our lives where angels played a major role in our assistance.

Chapter 8

Conclusion

Angels are very real spirit beings that come and go from heaven to earth mostly beyond the observation of people. They are our guardians that are here to help us with an extensive and varied ministry. They watch over all believers, protecting them from unseen dangers and evils. We activate this assistance through our prayers to the Lord, and our faith. We, of course, are never to pray to an angel, but it is our fervent prayers to God that will activate them to help us. Just because we can't see angels, doesn't mean they aren't helping us.

There is a whole world of unseen spirits both good and evil. While we know that Satan is against us, we also know that greater is He that is in us than he that is in the world. ("Ye are of God, little children, and have overcome them: because greater is He that is in you, than he that is in the world." 1 John 4:4, KJV) We can be sure that Satan will soon be defeated.

Questions about angels that remain a mystery.

If we could ask the Lord some questions about angels that are not answered in the Bible, what would they be? Here are some of my thoughts. Inquiring minds want to know!

How many angels are assigned to each person?

Exactly how many angels are there?

Is God finished creating angels or might He create more?

When a person dies, is their angel reassigned to a new born baby or do they continue to work with the person in heaven until they are acclimated and educated in the things of God.

How do they stop an accident or trouble from happening?

When they appear(ed) to people and look(ed) like a man, do they always look that way or are they just transformed for our benefit temporarily?

Do angels watch us from heaven most of the time or do they spend more time on earth near us? I ask this because of the Scripture that says their angels in heaven look down at us and see the face of the Father.

What do they do when they aren't helping us?

How much time off do they have to rest and do things they want to do?

Do they work in shifts so that there is sufficient time for rest and leisure?

Do they spend much time with people who have gone to heaven?

What kind of mansions or houses do they live in? Will their residences be intermingled with ours?

Since they are not a family-based community, do some of them live together in houses or does each one live alone?

How do they communicate with each other, with God, and how do they communicate with us in order to influence us to do good?

How long does it take for them to travel from heaven to earth in our timeframe?

How do they travel? Are they just mysteriously able to fly.

Since they had first-hand knowledge of God and all that He created, I would like to ask God how Satan and the fallen angels ever thought they might pull off dethroning Him.

Have the fallen angels, including Satan, ever had an opportunity to repent and turn back to God?

Did any of the good angels try to keep the foolish angels from taking the tragic step of falling away from God?

Why does God use angels to help us when He could do it Himself?

What kind of questions would you like to ask about angels? There are still so many fascinating facts about angels that we don't know. I'm sure in heaven our questions will all be answered.

I hope this exhaustive study has given us a clear understanding of the role of angels in the past, present, and future. I think we're all looking forward to meeting the angels in heaven, and finding out more about them. I think it will be most interesting to spend time with the angels that were assigned to us. I pray that this book has been a blessing to you!

"The angel of the Lord encamps around those who fear Him, and He delivers them."

Psalm 34:7

A Prayer

You may be interested in a sample prayer as follows:

Dear Heavenly Father,

Blessed be God, I have given and it is given to me, good measure, pressed down, shaken together, and running over. I have abundance and no lack. My God meets my needs according to His riches in glory. The Lord is my Shepherd, and I do not want. I say, in the name of Jesus that every disease germ, and virus that touches my body dies instantly.

No weapon formed against me will prosper, and whatever I do will prosper. I have the mind of Christ, and the wisdom of God is available to me. I am far from oppression. I have no fear of terror for it shall not come near me. We thank you, Lord, that the angels watch over us and protect us, because we have a loving Father who has provided this special help for us. All of this is extended to my family.

In Jesus Name, Amen.

A Salvation Prayer To Become Born Again

If you are not sure that you are ready to go to heaven, you can commit your life to Jesus Christ today.

A commitment to Christ requires a step of faith, an acceptance of the sacrifice, which He made for you. By dying on the Cross for us, Jesus has washed our sins clean with His blood.

Bible Readings

"If we confess our sins, He is faithful and just to forgive us our sins, and cleanse us from all unrighteousness."

1 John 1:9 (KJV)

"That if you confess with your mouth, 'Jesus is Lord,' and believe in your heart that God raised Him from the dead, you will be saved. For it is with your heart that you believe and are justified, and it is with your mouth that you confess and are saved."

Romans 10:9-10 (KJV)

"Therefore being justified by faith, we have peace with God through our Lord Jesus Christ."

Romans 5:1 (KJV)

If you are ready to make that commitment, and if you want to say "yes" to Jesus, then say the following prayer out loud:

Dear Jesus,

Thank you for the sacrifice You made for me. I am sorry for my past sins, and will try my best not to repeat them. I ask Your help to keep this pledge. I know I am not worthy but I willingly accept You as my Lord and Savior, and I thank You for Your blessing over my family and me. Please make me ready today to make heaven my eternal home. Thank you that today I am born again. Amen.

<u>Other Resources</u>

I have several books that have stories in them about people seeing and interacting with angels, as well as experiences in heaven. Perhaps you might be interested in this list of them.

Baker, H. A., *Visions Of Heaven,* Whitaker House, 1973.

Davis, Marietta, *Caught Up Into Heaven*, Whitaker House, 1999.

Sigmund, Richard, *A Place Called Heaven,* Lightfall Publishing, 2004.

Duplantis, Jesse, *Heaven: Close Encounters Of The God Kind*, Harrison House, 1996.

Springer, Rebecca Ruter, *My Dream of Heaven*: A Nineteenth Century Spiritual Classic (Originally Known as Intra Muros, 1898, (ISBN: 978-1577944706), Harrison House, 2002.

Lindsay, Gordon, *William Branham, A Man Sent From God*, William Branham.

Hunter, Charles and Frances, *Angels On Assignment*, Whitaker House, 1979.

Hagin, Kenneth E*., I Believe In Visions*, Kenneth Hagin Ministries, 1984.

Sabom, Michael, M.D., *Light & Death*, Zondervan Publishing House, 1998.

References

King James Version, referred to as KJV, B. B. Kirkbride Bible Co., Inc., 1964.

New International Version, referred to as NIV, Zondervan Bible Publishers, 1978.

Baker's Evangelical Dictionary of Biblical Theology. Edited by Walter A., Elwell, Baker Books, a division of Baker Book House, 1996.

Time Magazine, *Angels Among Us,* December 27, 1993.

Newsweek Magazine, *Angels,* December 27, 1993.

Fox News, *Mom Captures Daughter's Life-Saving Angel in Photograph,* December 24, 2008.

New York Times, *She Saw An Angel*, November 17, 1886.

Baker, H. A., *Visions Of Heaven,* Whitaker House, 1973.

Sabom, Michael, M.D., *Light & Death*, Zondervan Publishing House, 1998.

Hunter, Charles and Frances, *Angels On Assignment*, Whitaker House, 1979.

New York Times, *British Troops Say They Saw St. George*, October 17, 1915.

Other books by Niki Behrikis Shanahan

Who Says Animals Go To Heaven?

*A Collection Of Prominent Christian Leaders' Beliefs
In Life After Death For Animals.*

The Rainbow Bridge: Pet Loss Is Heaven's Gain

Pet loss support from a Christian perspective.

There Is Eternal Life For Animals

Proves through Bible Scripture that all animals go to Heaven.

Animal Prayer Guide

Prayers and blessings for your pet that you can use everyday.

You may order these titles by visiting us at
www.eternalanimals.com or contact the publisher at:

Niki Behrikis Shanahan

Pete Publishing

P. O. Box 282

Tyngsborough, MA 01879

Email: eternalanimals@comcast.net

We welcome you to visit us at:

www.eternalanimals.com